Blake Taylor's book, ADHD and Me, *is stereotype-busting from the outset. How can a whirlwind of a boy, now young man, like Blake, write such a lucid, disclosing, revealing, and, above all, insightful book? The book blends extremely personal descriptions of situations, binds, conflicts, and realities, some humorous and some deadly serious, with extremely useful practical information on how to cope with and overcome the often-devastating symptoms and impairments related to ADHD. Most of all, the book serves to humanize a label and a condition that are too frequently viewed with skepticism and even derision. This is a must-read for people of all ages who are concerned with ADHD, mental illness, treatment, coping, and stigma.*

—Stephen P. Hinshaw, professor and chair of the Department of Psychology at the University of California, Berkeley

Taylor offers readers an inside look at how he gets along on a daily basis as well as a guide for people in the same situation … Students struggling with ADHD and their parents will benefit from the author's insights.

—*Library Journal,* 15 November 2007

Taylor speaks to fellow teens and their families with an authority few experts can muster.

—*Publishers Weekly,* 17 November 2007

D0189254

ADHD & me

what i learned from lighting fires at the dinner table

blake e. s. taylor

CONTRA COSTA COUNTY LIBRARY

New Harbinger Publications, Inc.

I dedicate this book to:
my grandfather "Popop" and my grandmother Diana,
my great-grandmother Zaira, and
my mother Nadine.

Publisher's Note

This publication is designed to provide accurate and authoritative information in regard to the subject matter covered. It is sold with the understanding that the publisher is not engaged in rendering psychological, financial, legal, or other professional services. If expert assistance or counseling is needed, the services of a competent professional should be sought.

Distributed in Canada by Raincoast Books

Copyright © 2007 by Blake Taylor
New Harbinger Publications, Inc.
5674 Shattuck Avenue
Oakland, CA 94609
www.newharbinger.com

Cover and text design by Amy Shoup; Acquired by Tesilya Hanauer; Edited by Brady Kahn

---

Library of Congress Cataloging-in-Publication Data

Taylor, Blake E. S.
  ADHD and me : what I learned from lighting fires at the dinner table / Blake E.S. Taylor.
      p. cm.
  Includes bibliographical references.
  ISBN-13: 978-1-57224-522-8 (pbk. : alk. paper)
  ISBN-10: 1-57224-522-0 (pbk. : alk. paper)
  1. Taylor, Blake E. S.--Mental health. 2. Attention-deficit hyperactivity disorder--Patients--
California--Biography. I. Title.
RJ506.H9.T365 2007
618.92'85890092--dc22
[B]
                                          2007046473

10   09   08

10   9   8   7   6   5   4   3   2

contents

foreword

What a great gift *ADHD & Me* will be for teens going through this strug-gle and for parents hoping to glean tips and insights into their teens. I was struck most by Blake's courage and vulnerability in sharing some of the heartbreaking ups and downs of life as a teenager. I can see how the advice he shares and what he learned, if taken to heart, could keep a whole life from going down the wrong track.

The punch line of the book is the book itself. That a teenager with ADHD, once in a special ed class, is now an accomplished and published author is a testimonial to the substantial gifts of ADHD. *ADHD & Me* is an insider's look at being unpopular and bullied. And yet today, Blake is thriving and popular. These pages blaze forth with both the courage of brokenness and the power of self-improvement. His message of staging his own personal revolution in the service of constant self-improvement will inspire any teen or parent, even in the face of this diagnosis.

His book will help you translate the symptoms of ADHD into gifts as you see how they play out from the inside. Blake will show you how impulsiveness is often driven by intense curiosity, such as when he tells about breaking glass to see it shatter, lighting fires to see the flames, or shooting rockets with his grandfather because he liked seeing things fly. His perspective shows us how we miss the inventiveness and innovation when we focus too harshly on exploration gone wrong. One could easily imagine that Edison and Einstein had similar pratfalls in their teenage years in their unquenchable desire to see how the world works. Blake will walk you through his difficulties with concentration and show you how curiosity, adaptability, and interest in synthesizing across multiple domains can look like a crippling symptom when you are faced with a test based on straightforward memorization.

The one piece of advice that stands out and, to my mind, bears amplification is what he says about bullying. He urges teens to get help from adults. If you are a teen reading this book, or if you are a parent, this advice alone can do enough damage control to earn its keep on your bookshelf. I know that somewhere a teen will read Blake's story of seeking help and say, "What a geek!" If you have that reaction, check yourself—don't fall into the trap presented by the extremes that our culture goes to in enforcing its cowboy-like views on childhood. While most professionals urge parents and children to seek help from adults, the playground ethic and peculiarity of American culture tell us that even teenagers should be able to go it alone. This ideal of American independence for our kids and teens deepens teenage angst unnecessarily. Teachers need to be made aware of bullying, watch out for it, and stop it. It's as simple as that. Parents have to get schools involved and help their own child behind the scenes.

As with any literary narrative, Blake's story has a compelling subplot: the success of his mother Nadine as an advocate for him. Having met Blake and Nadine in person, her devotion and dedication to her child are palpable in her warmth and strength. In her personal account, she was challenged by many family members, friends, and teachers for her efforts to explain why Blake acted the way he did. She was accused of making excuses for him. Yet her efforts paid off. And she too is a heroine in the story, for this is what an ADHD child needs—a devoted advocate. If you are a parent reading this book, remember that you can in part change your child's reality when you go to bat for him or her and show others the bigheartedness that often lies behind your child's antics.

As a psychologist providing a guide to the reader, before you start with your shared journey with Blake, I would provide a few tips myself. Most important, in connecting with his story, or in places where you don't connect, I point to the context of his story.

If you are a teenager struggling with ADHD, you may wonder, "How could he write this book when I can't even find my assignment sheet?" An important part of the story's context is that Blake responded successfully to ADHD medications, and he had been on medications since the age of five. His story points to the effectiveness of the medications in managing symptoms and also to the great need that any ADHD child has for support and coaching, even with successful medication treatment. Getting rid of symptoms isn't enough. As Blake's story points out, even while he succeeded in school, the effects of the diagnosis dramatically affected his social life, his emotional life, and his whole image of how the world works and who he is. The debate that tears parents and families apart—to medicate or not to medicate—perhaps can recede to the background with this new revelation found in Blake's account. Success with medication is the very beginning of the story, not the end of the story.

Blake's story urges parents, teachers, and ADHD kids themselves to attend to the whole child. Too often, the diagnosis and treatment of these kids is about getting them to do well in school, getting them to remember their homework or follow directions. Even if these symptoms are treated with medications, there is whole child full of emotions, making his or her way through a world that is inclined to see differences as disorders, a whole child still in need of finding a direction in life. It is here, where medications leave off, in finding the gifts in ADHD—asking "what's right with my child?"—that parents can begin the real work of finding and building on strengths, rather than patching up weaknesses.

—Lara Honos-Webb, Ph.D.,
author of *The Gift of ADHD*

acknowledgments

I have many people to thank in life thus far. When I look back, I realize that all these people have had a hand in shaping me and my accomplishments.

I thank my mother, Nadine, who instinctively understands my true spirit and intelligence. She has been my teacher, advocate and protector. She encouraged me and helped me with ideas and the editing, research, and shaping of *ADHD & Me*.

I thank my father, Stan, for his sharp wit, his big bear hugs, our wrestling matches, working out together, our political discussions, and teaching me how to play golf.

I thank my grandmother Diana for babysitting me and allowing me to drive her crazy, for going with us to Hilton Head and making us stop at Cracker Barrel, and for the best shortbread cookies I've ever had; and "Popop," (my grandfather, Egildo) for the hundreds of hours he spent with me building wooden boats and race car tracks, setting up and playing with my Lionel trains, and launching rockets.

I thank my sister Madison, who has loved me intensely even though I have aggravated her since she was born by taking all her toys away. Now, we ski, swim, and team up together for online Roman battles. We are very close, and I love her deeply.

I thank my stepfather, Ben, who taught me about finance and organization and how to do formal presentations. He has patiently endured cable cars strung across the backyard and chemistry-experiments-in-a-bottle blowing up in his hands.

I thank Uncle Vinnie, my granduncle, who taught me about the stock market and how to save money, and who has been investing my savings for me in IBM, Merck, Exxon, and Pfizer since I was born.

I thank Papa T (my grandfather Samuel) for his stories about advancing across Europe while serving under General Patton in World War II, and for his stories about my grandmother Elvira, who died before I was born.

I thank these special people who are like family: Rhonda and Bill Wong (my unofficial godparents) for always being there, Lynne and Randy Bobson, Terry and Mercedes McCaffrey, and Mike Haydock who gave my mother the important book *Driven to Distraction* when I was little.

I thank the women who were like second mothers to me: Marjorie Maat from the Philippines and Gloria Marchan from Trinidad.

I thank our three greyhounds, Odette, Persephone, and Athena, and our former springer spaniels, Ashley and Becky, for loving me despite my faults.

I thank my doctors, Dr. Jean Paul Marachi, who I first saw when I was five years old and whose guidance has set the tone for my entire life, so far. Dr. Gerald Lieberman, who endured me screeching in his office every time he did a blood test and who told my mother not to worry, that I would turn out well despite my hyperactivity. Dr. Etta Bryant, who helped me through my move to California, and my years in middle school and high school.

I thank my principals and teachers, including Dr. Tomasello (Dr. T), former principal, Hurlbutt Elementary School, Weston, Connecticut, who took the time to have me do independent work with him in second grade, Claudia Manis, psychologist, and teachers Arlene Beckoff, Mark Tangerone, and Mrs. Motroni, my fifth grade teacher, who taught me the rigors of research and how to do presentations at a very early age.

At the Crocker Middle School, Hillsborough, California, I thank Janet Chun, principal, Susan Camarillo, counselor, Melanie Love, resource teacher, Troy Hager, daily TV news producer, and Lea Wedge Morrison, social studies teacher, who knew how to cultivate my talents.

I thank Tony Ignatius, concert pianist, who taught me to love classical piano, and who patiently endured our debates over interpretations of one Chopin Nocturne.

At the French American International High School in San Francisco, a rigorous, intellectual school, I thank Dan Harder, a terrific writer, who tutored me in IB essays and later read and edited my book chapters, and encouraged me to keep writing. I thank Andrew Brown, Richard Ulffers, and Betsy Brody for their faith in me. I thank Robert Stewart for encouraging me to pursue medicine as a career, Joel Cohen for teaching me chemistry, Netta Maclean for her four years of patience and for teaching me calculus, Dorothy Payne for opening my eyes to literature, and Armelle Courcelle-Labrousse and Katia Aouat, who made me fluent in French. I thank Ashley Rochman for her firm guidance during the college application process, and Stacie Rissman-Joyce, Leslie Adams, and Katrin McManus for helping me transition to high school.

I also thank my friends: Tony and his mother Kathy, who were my carpool "advisors" as I entered my new high school; Barbara, Matthew, Cindy, Lin, Pauline, Claire, Jo, Mike, Will, Laura (aka Bonnie), Eva (aka Zena), Stefan, Tommy, Chloe, Juliana, Sophie (aka Leaf), Keely, Graham, and, earlier, Danny, Ryan, and Luke for their moral support as friends.

I thank Tesilya Hanauer, associate acquisitions manager, New Harbinger Publications, who was kind enough to read and respond to an email from a sixteen-year old kid, and who has since endured my many questions, emails, and calls. Jess Beebe, senior editor and Brady Kahn, copy editor, for their critical suggestions.

I thank Carrie Cleinman, my mother's best friend from college, who took one look at me, identified my ADHD, and told my mother to take me to a doctor when I was five years old.

Finally, I thank Dr. Edward Jacobson who delivered me by emergency C-section—and saved my life.

introduction

tied to the kitchen chair 2nd grade

I am building a section of a robot on the family room floor. It is dinnertime, and Gloria, our babysitter, calls from the kitchen.

"Blakey, come back and sit down and eat, na!" Gloria coos to me in her singsong Trinidad accent. "You are eight years old. It is time to behave and eat yaw food."

I return to the table for one bite of steak. I chew it, then get up and leave the dinner table, again.

"Blake! Come and eat yaw dinner!" Gloria commands this time.

"I don't want to," I whine. I am thinking, "I don't want to sit down, and I have better things to do." I reluctantly return for another bite.

Finally, Gloria can't take it any more. She cooked this dinner and is determined to make me eat it. Frustrated, she takes a bungee cord and wraps it across my lap like a seatbelt. I struggle to escape, but being only eight, I'm not yet strong enough to do so. The steak is getting cold on its plate—it has been on the dinner table for an hour—and I have been continually leaving the table to play with my K'nex and Legos on the family room floor.

There is a pause for a minute or so. Madison, my five-year-old sister, looks across the table in shock. She looks at the bungee cord and then at Gloria standing behind me. I listen to the background noise of the television broadcasting Gloria's favorite late afternoon show: *Oprah*.

Finally, I give in and relax my body. I reluctantly eat the last pieces of meat. With the help of Gloria and her bungee cord, I am actually able to sit still long enough to finish dinner.

living with ADHD

I have lived with attention-deficit/hyperactivity disorder (ADHD) for my entire life—all seventeen years of it. I'm one of approximately four million young people in the United States who has ADHD (CDC 2005). I'm keenly aware of how I am different. I see things differently. I experience sights and sounds more keenly. I react more intensely. I can still look back and vividly remember what happened to me in preschool and elementary school and middle school, because those times are not so long ago and because the memories—the humor and sometimes the pain—are clearly etched in my mind. Now that I am seventeen years old, I can tell you about what is still happening to me as a teenager. I wanted to write about ADHD and me. This is my story. But with a few changes of places and people, it could also be *your story*.

Have some of the following things happened to you—have you gotten into such predicaments with parents, teachers, and friends? I know what it feels like when your mother gets really angry because you are just having fun shooting pebbles in the yard and accidentally shatter the sliding glass door. Or your father calls you disrespectful because you answer back, trying to defend yourself. Or your sister calls you "clueless" because you don't get the joke that everyone else is laughing at. Or your teacher singles you out for punishment because she figures you had to be the culprit, even though you didn't do it. Or when you have nervous tics and your schoolmates glare at you. Or when your friend doesn't call to go bicycling, even though he promised he would.

Guess what. You are not alone. You are not unusual. You just have ADHD. All of us are facing the very same things. And there are a lot of things we can do. First, we need to understand what makes us different, and, second, we need to realize what we can do about it—and how we can use ADHD's gifts for a wonderful advantage! You don't need to *apologize* about ADHD; you just need to learn how to use it.

Perhaps I should start with a little background about myself. I was born on May 25, 1989, at 3:12 P.M. in Greenwich, Connecticut. I lived in Weston, Connecticut (approximately a twenty-five minute drive from Greenwich, one and a half hours north of New York), with my father, Stan (whom I call "P"), and my mother, Nadine (whom I nicknamed "Mimi"). My maternal grandparents Diana and Egildo (called "Grandma" and "Popop") and Uncle Vinnie were a constant presence in our lives. They came to visit us every Saturday. First, we would all have milk, coffee, and crumb cake together, and then I would build with Popop or garden with Uncle Vinnie. I had many buffet dinners with Papa T, my paternal grandfather, and old-fashioned Thanksgiving dinners with my uncles Milton and Saul and aunts Lisa and Mary. When I was three, I began going to pre-school at the Weston Westport Cooperative Nursery School, and later I attended the Hurlbutt Elementary School.

In 1992, my sister Madison was born, and my mother took a leave of absence from IBM so she could spend time reading to us and taking us to apple orchards and museums. Later, when my mother returned to work, she hired Gloria, a caring black woman from Trinidad, to help look after my sister and me. My parents were often out of the house throughout the 1990s. My father worked hard building his furniture store business, and my mother worked as a global communications manager for IBM in New York, and so we would rarely have family dinners together.

When I was five, I went with my mother to one of her Vassar College reunions, at which her best friend, Carrie, took one look at me running around Lathrop dorm and told my mother I had ADHD and that she should take me to a specialist as soon as possible. My mother took me to see Dr. Jean Paul Marachi, who became my doctor for many years. He diagnosed me with ADHD as I entered kindergarten at Hurlbutt. Dr. Marachi advised my parents and teachers how to guide and help me. He first prescribed dexedrine for my ADHD, and then he moved me to Adderall because I needed a longer-lasting medicine. Adderall worked extremely well, and I took it for the next ten years.

In fourth grade, when I began middle school at Weston Middle School, I developed tics. These included whirling tics and vocal tics, which came and went. Dr. Marachi prescribed a clonidine patch, along with my Adderall, to reduce the tics. It was also during middle school that my parents divorced.

In 2000, my mother married my stepfather, Ben (whom I affectionately refer to as "the Czar"), an executive at IBM. However, almost immediately after their marriage, Ben was offered a key job in California during the dot-com era. Since the new position enabled my mother to stay home with my sister and me, we decided to move to California. I was in the middle of sixth grade at this time, and I was reluctant to move three thousand miles west, where my father had warned me of earthquakes and mudslides. My grandparents were upset that we were leaving the New York area. As my grandmother said, "Why would anyone want to leave New York?" Since Gloria could not move with us, I had to say good-bye to the woman who had been like a second mother to me. On November 30, 2000, we moved to a suburb south of San Francisco. I attended William Crocker Middle School, a public school.

I managed to deal with the distance by talking daily to my father and weekly to my grandparents and by visiting Connecticut during summers and other vacations. My father and grandparents came out during the months I could not go back. As my mother said, "Just because you moved from Connecticut doesn't mean you leave it behind. It is always a part of you." Also, I kept in contact with my friends through IM and Facebook.

In 2002, Marjorie, a hardworking and dedicated woman from the Philippines, became our babysitter and joined us in many family predicaments.

In 2003, when Strattera, a nonstimulant ADHD medication, came out, my new doctor, Dr. Etta Bryant, changed my prescription, and I have been taking this medicine ever since.

After attending my eighth-grade graduation, my grandfather Popop died suddenly in June after having visited us in California. It was a crushing blow to lose my best friend and accomplice. In September, I began high school at the French-American International School in San Francisco, where one hears French as often as English and where I experienced city life, learned how to handle mass transit, and developed longtime friends. I began writing this book during the summer of 2005, when I was sixteen. I am now attending the University of California at Berkeley where I plan to major in Biology and Chemistry.

glossary of names

Aki—my former best friend in Connecticut (not his real name)

Brian—a friend of mine in sixth grade

The Czar—my stepfather, Ben

Gloria—my Trinidadian babysitter when I lived in Connecticut

Grandma—my grandmother Diana

Madison—my sister

Marjorie—our Filipina babysitter in California

Matt—a longtime friend of mine from middle school

Mimi—nickname for my mother, Nadine

Mr. Martin–my physical education teacher at Crocker Middle School

Mrs. Perril–my first-grade teacher in Connecticut (not her real name)

Mrs. Sellars–my tenth-grade English teacher

Nadine–my mother

Netta–my high school math teacher

Phillip–a bully in sixth grade (not his real name)

Popop–my grandfather Egildo

Stan–my father

Uncle Vinnie–my granduncle

Will–a high school friend

being distracted

the odyssey 10th grade

I wake up, reluctantly, at 6:10 A.M. to get ready for school. Being December, the sun has not yet risen, and so I'm frustrated that I have to get up so early to commute to my high school twenty miles away in San Francisco.

Since it's the Christmas season, stores, restaurants, and the neighborhoods are festive with multicolored lights, Santa Clauses, and angel figures. However, I hardly feel like celebrating, because this is tenth grade and it's finals week. I have finals in each of my subjects, and today I will take the two-hour English exam, which consists of writing a lengthy in-class essay. This essay, as my English teacher, Mrs. Sellars, has told us, will be on *The Odyssey*, by Homer.

After finishing my morning routine, I eat a ham-and-cheese omelet. Heavy on the protein—which I've read is good for people with ADHD. As I eat, I think about the upcoming exam and my reluctance to sit and write an essay for two hours.

My mother is driving the carpool to school, so I rush to get all my things together so we won't be late picking up my carpool mate Tony. We are a few miles from home before I realize that I've forgotten something: to take my ADHD medicine. Normally, I would not consider this a cause for concern, because the medication that I take—Strattera—has a lasting effect and remains in your system for a period of time. Today, however, is not the day to miss my medication or to be even slightly inattentive or distracted. I need every bit of attention to master this English exam, especially since English is not one of my favorite subjects. It's a struggle to stay focused on the material even on regular days. Despite this thought, though, I choose not to tell my mother about forgetting the medicine, because I don't want her to chide me for twenty-five minutes while I'm captive in the car as we drive to school.

As we approach the French-American International School, the winter sun is now above the horizon. It is unusually sunny for this time of year; normally there's a gray blanket of fog and drizzle nestled around the school in central San Francisco.

I go into the main entrance of the school and then into the elevator. My teacher, Mrs. Sellars, is standing inside, and we greet each other. She is an older, short blonde woman with thick eyeglasses and a nervous, birdlike manner. She clutches a packet of papers with the school's logo on them.

"Is the test hard today?" I ask, half smiling, not expecting a real answer.

"Well, I guess you'll find out. Let's hope you were paying attention in class." She studies me. She doesn't think that I've paid attention in class or that I take English seriously. Actually, even though I struggle with English literature, I studied long hours over the weekend for this test.

I swallow hard. The thought of a potentially disastrous grade on my final exam enters my mind; I know I am a lot more vulnerable to distraction without my medication. I've learned over the years that the medication has to remain at a certain level in my bloodstream to be effective—especially when I'm going into a final exam.

The elevator stops at the fifth floor, and I exit. Some of my fellow classmates, who were out partying last weekend instead of studying for finals, huddle nervously together, attempting to cram for the final. They plead with their friends for a general overview of *The Odyssey*, Homer's epic poem about the Greek hero Odysseus, who traveled the Aegean Sea for ten years trying to get home to Ithaca. But I've been serious about trying to get a good grade in English, and I'm confident that I've studied enough. I am, however, very concerned that my ADHD will cause a problem during the exam.

The supervising teacher begins to announce the English exam rooms. He announces our class first: "Mrs. Sellars 10 English: Room 535" in a French accent.

After hesitating for a moment, I enter the classroom with my *Odyssey* book and am shocked by the explosion of color and artwork that decorates the room. It's ablaze with color. Normally, I would be content to be in a room decorated with art, but this is my final exam. It counts for 25 percent of my grade, and I desperately need to be able to concentrate solely on writing the paper.

I sit next to a window for fresh air, and the proctor distributes the exams to the fifteen students in the room. "Alors, nous allons commencer l'éxamen en deux minutes." *Okay, we are going to start the exam in two minutes*, he announces in French. In my school, you hear as much French as English.

"Ça va tout le monde? Est-ce que quelqu'un a besoin d'un crayon ou d'un stylo?" *Is everyone okay? Does anyone need a pencil or pen?*" No one answers.

"Commencez." *Begin.*

> I've been serious about trying to get a good grade in English, and I'm confident that I've studied enough. I am, however, very concerned that my ADHD will cause a problem during the exam.

I turn over the exam and read the essay topic: "Discuss the role of the goddess Circe in *The Odyssey* and the metaphorical purpose of turning men into pigs."

"An easy question," I think to myself. I know all about Circe, the beautiful goddess on the Greek island of Aeaea who turned Odysseus's men into swine. I also know how to connect her to the themes and motifs of *The Odyssey*. But only a few minutes after I begin to develop my ideas, there's a problem.

Since the day is relatively pleasant, a hundred or so elementary school children from the lower school are out in the playground five stories below. They start playing kickball ("Shoot it in the goal!") and hide-and-seek ("Go hide, Mary! He's coming!"). They scream and yell, "Get the ball away from him!" The window is open, and the shrill noise pierces my ears.

"Blake, est-ce que tu peux fermer la fenêtre s'il te plaît?" *Blake, can you close the window, please?* The proctor asks me in order to reduce the noise.

"D'accord." *Okay,* I reply.

For a moment, I think the closed window will muffle the noise, but as I return to my desk, there is still a steady trickle of noise filtering through the window. "Here, pass the ball. Time out!" Bells, whistles, screams, people running up and down the stairs.

After ten minutes of trying to concentrate and trying not to be distracted by the noise the kids are making outside, I've written only one sentence about Circe: *"The goddess had invited the men into her parlor and she let them feast on cheese and wines and grain. Slowly, they began turning into pigs."* I have one hour and ten minutes left to complete the essay. I look around the class. My classmates have simply tuned out the noise and are writing furiously on their papers. But not me. I am looking at the posters on the classroom walls, at the sun on the windowpane.

I try to remember instances in the epic where I can connect Circe and her wicked deeds to their thematic importance, but it's difficult, because the noise of the kids outside stays in the forefront of my mind and hinders my ability to think. I become frustrated.

In an attempt to calm myself, I look at the walls and intricate details of the artwork that students in the class have created, and think to myself how I would much rather be painting or sculpting than writing an English essay: self-portraits, still lifes, landscapes.

There are also maps of Europe on the walls. One of the maps shows the borders during and after the First World War and points out where key battles took place. Under each battle, there is a number that correlates to a legend on the bottom of the map describing the major events of the battle. I start to read some quite interesting details about terrible gas attacks and how thousands of soldiers died from suffocation. Suddenly, I remember that I have to write the English essay. I now have only fifty minutes left, with only a paragraph written on my paper.

As I force myself to come up with ideas about Circe *"Odysseus was aided by the god Hermes and found the herb moly, which had the power to counteract the drug Circe had given to his men,"* I envy the freedom that the children have outside and the fact that they won't have to face a final exam like this for years—until they enter high school.

Then I think about how I too could be free doing my favorite summer activity, sailing. I want to captain a catamaran, a sailboat with two hulls, since it can go into the shallow waters of the San Francisco Bay. However, at the sailing camp where I have learned to sail, they have only single-hull sailboats—420s and FJs—so I can't rent a catamaran. Unfortunately, it's winter, and it wouldn't be warm enough to sail.

I then think about winter sports and how I love skiing at Squaw Valley at Lake Tahoe. I think about slalom racing down the packed powder, cold dry air on my face. Edging, cutting, sending up plumes of snow, speeding by people on the mountain. But, oh god! I still have to write this essay! My mind is flitting around uncontrollably.

With only a half hour remaining, I force my sweating hand to write as fast as possible. *"Circe was directed by the Gods to take care of Odysseus and his men. She invited them to stay on her island. They stayed for a year and they feasted every day. But eventually they were eager to travel home, and Circe told them they had to visit the house of Hades, the god of the underworld, before they could go on."* My ideas, I know, are not fully developed, because I can't concentrate. Ironically, the distractions remind me of Circe. The distractions, like Circe, entice you and beckon to you to daydream and enjoy yourself, but in the process of doing so, you become a pig (like Odysseus's men)—and, in this case, you run out of time to complete your English essay.

When the proctor announces that the time for the essay is over, I hand in my incomplete paper, knowing full well that my fears have been realized.

After the Christmas break, I go to meet with Mrs. Sellars to collect my final exam and discuss my grade. After we greet each other and ask how the holidays were spent, she pulls out my paper. She has it folded lengthwise, as she always does with our essays and exams.

"So, how did I do?" I ask, trying to be optimistic, but I know that the grade will not be favorable.

"Umm..." she begins her thought. I search her face for a hint of a smile—perhaps a slight wrinkle on the edge of her mouth—but can find none.

"Not that well, actually," she replies reluctantly as she glances at my paper. She is obviously annoyed with me. She is probably thinking, "Another smart-ass kid. Not wanting to apply himself. Not wanting to do the work."

"Oh..." My heart begins pounding quickly. I feel my face beginning to flush. I feel angry with myself for being so forgetful about my medicine on exam day. I look at the back of the paper, hoping to see the outline of the grade and hoping that it will at least be reasonably acceptable. But as I turn the page over, the grade is clear: D.

I have never gotten a D! I begin to worry about my mother's reaction. I begin to worry about how I will get through the rest of tenth-grade English—and then eleventh- and twelfth-grade English. I begin to worry about how a bad grade in English will affect my chances of getting into college. Will I even be accepted into college? My future prospects are evaporating before my eyes.

"You just didn't go in-depth enough; perhaps next time you will improve," Mrs. Sellars says in a relaxed tone. How could she be so relaxed when my future is at stake?

"It's just that I was overwhelmed by distractions during the test," I answer.

She feigns a smile to acknowledge that she has heard my comment, but I can easily see that she doesn't believe a word of it. Behind her smile, I can tell that she is thinking, "I've heard all types of excuses before about why students didn't do well on exams, but this excuse is a new one." She raises an eyebrow.

As far as I know, Mrs. Sellars was informed at the beginning of the year about the fact that I have ADHD, but she doesn't believe it's an excuse to not do well on an exam.

"You see," I continue, trying to explain and to convince her, "I studied for this exam all weekend. I'm supposed to take my ADHD medication daily, but because I was nervous on the morning of the exam, I forgot to take it. And so I couldn't concentrate." I feel like I am drowning in my own words and that my excuses are futile.

Mrs. Sellars looks at me incredulously. Her eyes examine every corner of my face, searching for the slightest hint of dishonesty. Now I regret how I have disrupted her class many times, kidding around, not paying attention, and getting my classmates to laugh. My classroom antics are coming back to haunt me in a big way. I don't blame her for not believing me.

I leave her office despondent and irate at myself. I should have known better. I should have been more careful about taking my medication. All my work, all my studying for the final, has been for nothing. My teacher doesn't even believe me! But the fact of the matter is that even though I try to fight it, being distracted has been a significant problem that I've had to deal with over and over again.

cause & effect

Distraction—or lack of attention—is one of the most common and obvious symptoms of ADHD. In fact, this inability to focus—not paying attention to a teacher, not following instructions on a math test, not being able to stay focused on your social studies homework—is usually one of the ways that

ADHD is first identified in young people. All the ADHD medications attempt to correct distraction or inattention so that kids can follow parents' and teachers' directions:

"Don't forget your math book."

"Take your lunch money."

"Let the dog out."

"Pay attention in class."

"Compare and contrast the characters in the book *Pride and Prejudice*—don't do a summary of the book."

When those of us with ADHD are able to listen and comprehend what is being said to us, we can do our homework, study for tests, and, perhaps, even make our beds.

I believe that distraction results from an inability to concentrate. When you can't focus, your mind wanders to anything—and everything—around you. And your mind continues wandering, flitting from object to object. It can be an open window, a bird chirping, music from a radio, a bright color on someone's shirt, a conversation in the other room, or a ray of light on a bookcase.

Distraction occurs for a variety of reasons. The major cause is that the physical wiring of the ADHD brain is different from the average brain. When I say "wiring," it is not actually wires, of course, but chemicals operating in and among the nerve cells—specialized cells that carry electrical signals to and from the brain and within the brain. For example, you may say to yourself, "Listen to Mrs. Sellars describe the Cyclops Polyphemus." The signal must jump from one nerve cell to another in order to progress along its path to ultimately carry out the "listen" order. Special chemicals, known as neurotransmitters, carry or ferry the signal from one nerve cell to the next. In ADHD brains, there aren't enough of the special neurotransmitters to carry the signals between nerve cells, and so the signals stop prematurely (Zeigler Dendy, and Zeigler 2003; Walker 2005). As a result, the order—"to listen about Polyphemus"—doesn't get transmitted or fulfilled and doesn't happen.

Doctors say that because of the signals stopping along their path, ADHD brains are less able to distinguish between what is relevant (to listen to your teacher) and what is irrelevant (the sound of kids playing). The function of ADHD medication, therefore, is to correct this problem and allow the mind to filter out unimportant data (Walker 2005). I hear Mrs. Sellars talking about Odysseus blinding the Cyclops—an important fact—but then I am thinking about my classmate Cindy and what she said to Lin, that Stephen is wearing a shirt that doesn't go with his pants, that two students outside the classroom door are talking about who danced with whom at a party last Saturday night. I cannot stop the other sights, sounds, and thoughts from flooding into my brain and competing for my attention. These other stimuli are competing with what Mrs. Sellars is saying about Odysseus's men clinging to the underbelly of the sheep to escape the Cyclops. So, in effect, although I hear every word she says, I comprehend only part of what she is saying.

> When distraction—and therefore the inability to concentrate—occurs, I feel as if my mind were a television with the channel changing uncontrollably.

The ADHD medicines help alleviate this problem. Scientists are not exactly sure how they help, but they guess that these medications enable you to pay attention because they provide chemicals that allow the brain signals to flow uninterrupted from neuron to neuron. Dr. Russell Barkley, a renowned expert on ADHD, said there are some signs "that the stimulants are achieving an increase in the amount of dopamine that is within the synapses between brain cells—those critical gaps between brain cells where the neurotransmitters are supposed to do their work" (PBS Frontline 2007). As a result, you can carry out the command to listen to your teacher. Of course, if you don't *want* to listen because you don't like epic poetry, that's a different story. The medicines will, however, help you listen if you want to do so.

When distraction—and therefore the inability to concentrate—occurs, I feel as if my mind were a television with the channel changing uncontrollably. In one moment, I'm watching *CNN Headline News,* in another moment, a documentary about the Roman army, and in a third moment, *What Not to Wear* on TLC.

For instance, one evening in seventh grade, I wanted to do my homework and read about the Austrian Archduke Ferdinand, but then I decided to Google the city of Trieste in northern Italy, which had been surrendered to Italy after World War I. My great-grandmother Zaira's family, who were Austrian, had lived in Trieste. I started reading about the city, and then, instead of doing the assigned book report, I decided to make a small binder for my grandmother about the history of Trieste.

Another time, while I was running for president of eleventh grade, I would spend my chemistry, math, and English classes creating advertising posters for my campaign (I lost by a slim margin) instead of doing work. Sometimes on a Saturday afternoon, I'll decide to lift weights, but then by the time I lift the first dumbbells, I suddenly realize that I would rather watch television, and ten minutes or so into the TV program, I decide I feel like building something. Eventually, I begin to wander aimlessly around the house, looking for something on which to settle. However, as I exhaust all the possibilities of an activity, I become bored. If I am doing an assignment—even without the time constraints of a final exam—distraction can still strike. I could be writing an essay, for example, and then begin to do other tasks instead. Distraction thus can lead to either procrastination or to boredom.

Interestingly, although ADHD inhibits ordinary concentration, it can surprisingly enable you to hyperfocus—a type of extreme concentration

> Hyperfocus is the opposite of distraction, but these two states are not mutually exclusive. I can be, in one moment, distracted, and then suddenly I can be hyperfocused, doing my work unimpeded.

during which you can block out any and all sensory impressions. It is a unique ability. Hyperfocus is the opposite of distraction, but these two states are not mutually exclusive. For example, I can be, in one moment, distracted, and then suddenly, in another moment, I can be hyperfocused, doing my work unimpeded. Time will fly by as I perform the best at my studies. I once worked on a project about racing greyhound rescue work and adoption and spent eight hours straight writing the report.

I made a D on my Homer essay because I was too distracted to write effectively—but it wasn't the end of my academic career. In many later final exams, when I took my medicine I found that I was able to successfully concentrate on the tests, complete my thoughts, make the connections, and finish the essays.

⟳ solutions

There are several key ways to prevent distraction. The following techniques work for me. Try them.

① **Be organized.** Organization leads to clear thoughts that prevent distraction. If your desk, books, papers, pens, pencils, binders, and so on are organized, your thoughts will be more structured and more clear, because your inner thought process reflects the outside environment. This is why many people find being on a quiet beach mentally soothing.

When I study for final exams or do homework, I go to the dining room table with all the items I need to study and neatly lay them out in a regular, gridlike fashion on the table. As a result, my capacity to absorb the information in the textbooks increases, and my thoughts are more structured because the materials are organized. When I prepare for a project, I mentally plan the sections of the project I must complete, with due dates for each phase until the final due date. During tests, before I answer a question, I organize my thoughts first, rather than just jump in. During my English exams, for example, I usually create a detailed outline of what points I want to address, so when I write on the actual exam paper, I simply turn the ideas already on paper into complete sentences. Work and studying become easier when you're organized. This will encourage you to continue being more organized.

(2) **Create a distraction-free environment.** It is important to create an environment that is simple and soothing. Do not create a background with bright colors, pictures, and decorations, because this will easily distract your eye. On the other hand, avoid working in a blank, white-walled room; it helps to have something pleasant to stare at in order to generate thoughts. Your workspace should be mildly interesting, but not so interesting that it distracts you.

(3) **Work in a quiet room.** People with ADHD are much more sensitive to noises than those without the condition. Some common examples of distracting noises are cars honking, dogs barking, and little children shrieking. I am not suggesting that you work in a *completely* quiet room; generally it is better to hear soft music playing, birds chirping, or soothing ocean sounds, for instance. A good indicator of the balance between too much and too little noise is that if you start paying attention to the noise, it's too loud. My mother is convinced that classical music organizes my mind and helps me relax and think. When I study for tests or finals, I do so in a subtly decorated room with light classical music in the background.

(4) **Be well rested and take breaks.** Being tired causes you to be more distracted because it takes a lot of effort to concentrate. So, get your sleep and take breaks (Graham 2006). Everyone who works needs breaks, but to those with ADHD, breaks are vital. It is important that you do not exhaust your mental energy during a final exam. If you are stumped by an

idea or at a new question in the test, go to the water fountain for a few minutes to allow your mind to recuperate. However, do not overuse the concept of taking a break; it will interrupt your train of thought and you will squander your time. When I study at home, for instance, I prioritize my list, decide what I need to accomplish, and then promise myself a break as a reward. I take a five-minute break every half hour or so. During the break, I play the piano, eat a snack such as cheese and crackers, run after the dog, or annoy my sister by going on her IM account.

(5) **Take your medicine.** Don't do what I did on the day of my final exam on *The Odyssey*. Religiously take your medicine. It gives you a good base from which to operate.

(6) **Find a routine or pattern of study.** Routines are good for your body as well as for your mind. Just as it's good to have a routine before bedtime, it's good to have a routine for study. Routines reinforce what you're trying to do. If you set up a pattern, you are training your mind to think, "Okay, now I am getting ready to study."

Create a place and a routine that work for you and enable you to concentrate. You'll be amazed at what you can accomplish. Discovering what works for me has been my own personal odyssey!

being impulsive

lighting fires at the dinner table 9th grade

The doorbell rings at 6:30 P.M. I briskly climb the wooden stairs from my downstairs room, skipping every other step as usual. The black flip-flops I'm wearing fall off my feet toward the top of the stairs, so reluctantly I pick them up.

As I approach the front door, the shadow of my friend Matt is barely visible behind the partially tinted glass door. The Christmas lights twinkle outside.

We go downstairs to my room. As usual, he sits on my futon, and I lie down on my bed. Just then, Marjorie, our sitter from the Philippines, announces that dinner is ready.

Matt and I run upstairs to the kitchen. The hood over the stove is thundering and there is the crisp smell of teriyaki chicken in the air. As we walk in, Marjorie is cleaning a wooden rice spoon.

Pointing the spoon at us, she says, "Okay, you go there and eat now."

We turn and walk toward the neatly set table. My twelve-year-old sister, Madison, is almost finished with her bowl of teriyaki chicken and rice, and she looks bored.

Madison looks at Matt and makes a weird face at him. Matt and I exchange looks. Madison giggles. She has nothing to do. After scanning the kitchen for a minute, looking for something to play with, she locks her eyes on the refrigerator. She goes over to the refrigerator, opens it, and pulls out a container of yogurt. Uninterested, I look away and put a piece of chicken in my mouth. Madison returns to the table with not only the yogurt but also a lighter in her hand. Matt looks at me ominously.

"Okay, yogurt, it's time to die," My sister addresses the yogurt as she flicks the lighter on.

About a minute later, Madison manages to light a small flame at the edge of the yogurt container, creating a faint odor of burning plastic. Matt looks at Madison as if she needs to be committed. Marjorie continues cleaning dishes, her back to us and to the flame. Classical music drones on in the background, along with the sound of running water from the kitchen sink.

Just then, an idea comes into my head. I see the fire burning on the yogurt casing and the motion of the flame. I don't think about how stupid it is to have a yogurt container burning on the kitchen table. In fact, I don't think at all about the danger of fire. Instead, I think of chemistry lab and how we purposely light things on fire to find their ignition points. But I am not thinking of controls or safety procedures, which would be part of a proper

> I don't think about how stupid it is to have a yogurt container burning on the kitchen table. Instead, I think of chemistry lab and how we purposely light things on fire to find their ignition points.

chemistry experiment, done in a chemistry lab. I only think of lighting something—anything—on fire to see what will happen.

I stand up, walk across the kitchen, and open the medicine cabinet. Inside is Bactine, Band-Aids, gauze—the usual first-aid collection. I scan the cabinet for a flammable fluid. I find it in a blue-gray bottle labeled "eyeglass cleanser."

Giddy with the excitement of the moment, I walk across the kitchen toward where Madison is reigniting the yogurt container with the lighter. It is a small candle-sized flame, but it won't be small for long. As I approach the flame, I open the eyeglass cleanser bottle and pour it on the yogurt.

In a millisecond, the small flame flares upward into a blaze. Frightened, I automatically throw the bottle onto the table. The red-orange flame, which now engulfs half of the kitchen table, traces the trajectory of the flying bottle and its flammable liquid in the air. Madison runs for water. Matt jumps away from the table. I am in shock, paralyzed.

Marjorie suddenly sees the reflection of the huge flame in the window at the sink. She turns around and screams.

I shriek, "Marjorie, get the water!"

I pick up a glass pitcher filled with lemonade and throw the lemonade at the flame. This helps, but the flame still surges around the table. After burning through the eyeglass cleanser fluid, the flame leaps onto one of the white chair seats and to the red rug underneath the table. Marjorie fills a large cooking pot with water and splashes it on the table and on the seat.

"The rug. The rug!" Madison shouts. The rug is burning.

Matt jumps on the flame on the rug and extinguishes it. The fire is over. Luckily, no one is hurt. I am saved. Light smoke swirls and hangs in the kitchen air for a few quiet seconds.

Just then, the house fire alarm goes off. It is a shrill, incessant, loud noise.

"Oh no! Not the alarm!" I cry. I know I am in serious trouble now.

My mother comes running out of her bedroom, dressed in a blue-and-yellow-flowered bathrobe. My stepfather follows her. They've been getting ready for a neighbor's Christmas party.

"What is going on here?" my mother screams, seeing the water and the smoke around the kitchen table. She looks at me. "Blake! What happened?"

"Blake! Answer your mother," says my stepfather.

Pointing at me, Marjorie blurts out, "He pour da bottle with da fire, and I look around and dere is dis big flame, you know, and he say, 'Marjorie help!'" Her English is broken because she is so upset.

Before my mother can respond, sirens wail and lights flash outside, illuminating the whole front of our house. A huge truck screeches to a stop. Yes, the fire department has arrived. Our alarm is connected to the fire department, so when it goes off, they are immediately alerted.

My heart is beating fast, and I'm sweating profusely. I begin to realize the seriousness of what I've done and the fact that the authorities will now know about it also. I have almost set the house on fire because of my impulsivity.

The firemen knock on the door. The Christmas lights flash in unison with the police and fire truck lights outside.

"Blake, come here now!" My mother orders as she fixes her wet hair behind her ears. The alarm is shrieking.

"I am truly sorry, sir…" my mother exclaims to the firemen. My mother always ends up apologizing to people because of my actions. "We doused the fire."

The firemen march in to check the house. They scan the ceilings for signs of smoke, and then they fan out in separate directions to check all the rooms, as they are supposed to do when there is a fire. They want to hear what happened, and then they want to talk to me on my own.

I am left alone with the firemen.

"What happened?"

"Why did you put flammable liquid on a flame?"

"Did you know that the fire would flare up? That it could have burned all of you?"

"Do you understand that the fire could have burned down the entire house?"

My answers do not make sense and only prompt more questions. It is because I don't really have a good answer. "Why did I do this?" I ask myself. I am not really sure. Was it for the excitement? I promise the firemen I will never act so irresponsibly again. And I mean it.

The firemen and the police finally leave. I think to myself, "This will be an event that will pass, and we will laugh about later." Or so I hope. But no one is laughing now.

I return to the kitchen. The yogurt is muddy and blackened, and the wooden floor is covered in a thick layer of smoke dust. The seat of the chair is partially burnt, and the rug is charred.

My mother calls me into her room. I dread the display of emotion that is coming. She is crying as she explains what could have happened.

"You could have been burned and maimed for life; your sister could have been burned, Marjorie, Matt,... the house, everything we own. This is fire, Blake, fire." It is a blur of words.

"But Madison started it," I blurt out. And then I think of how ridiculous the excuse sounds. Am I blaming my younger sister for my impulsive behavior?

My mother tears into my words, "Madison started it. Is *that* what you have to say? And you had to finish it!" Now her anger starts.

"Did it occur to you to stop your sister when you saw her doing something like this? That you are three years older and that you should have more sense? Did it occur to you to stop the fire and not add to it?"

There is another blur of words, and then the next statement stuns me. It seems so out of context.

"And you can forget about driving," my mother says.

My heart sinks. I am going to be turning sixteen the following May, and I, just like all the other kids my age, want to start learning how to drive.

"This was impulsive and irresponsible," my mother says. "How could we possibly trust you with a car? You can forget about driving for a long time."

My mother feels too sick to her stomach to go to the Christmas party. My sister, who is supposed to go to the party to be with her friend, is grounded for her role in inciting me and is sent to her room. My mom calls Matt's father and asks him to pick Matt up—as a means of punishing me. And I am sent into isolation in my room for the rest of the weekend. I am not to come out of my room. My meals will be brought to me.

cause & effect

It is well-known that impulsivity is one of the more negative characteristics associated with ADHD. Fortunately, not everyone with ADHD is impulsive, but many boys and young men with ADHD are impulsive (National Resource Center on ADHD 2007). I, for one, have been impulsive my entire life, and it has taken different forms. There was the fire incident, and before that, I had a driving desire to shoot at objects, which I'd been doing ever since I was two years old. In middle school, I created a slingshot by stringing thirty rubber bands across the handle of my rolling backpack. I once hit a teacher's behind. Another time, when walking home from school, I hit and shattered the back window of a green Cadillac. At home, I shattered the glass patio door twice with pebbles. This instinct, when mixed with impulsivity, is a recipe for trouble.

You are probably wondering if I got into trouble. Yes, I got into trouble. The slingshot was taken away, and I would be sent to my room, not allowed to watch TV, or not allowed on the computer. After the punishment was served, however, I would make another slingshot and continue shooting pebbles.

I didn't mean to shatter the glass. At the time, I was thinking of how entertaining it would be to see flying pebbles. A person with ADHD often does not think about cause and effect, does not connect the dots between thought, action, and consequence. You shoot pebbles because you want to see them fly, and you don't think about the objects in their path. The pebbles hit the windows, people get angry, and you get yelled at, and you don't understand why you are getting yelled at, because all you were trying to do was see the flying pebbles. These all seem like independent—and unrelated—events in your mind.

Dr. Russell Barkley, a doctor who devoted his entire career to studying ADHD, said that when you are impulsive, you can't stop and think before you act, that you say and do things without thinking about what is going to happen (PBS Frontline 2007). In my case, I was so busy with the slingshot that it overrode my common sense—that little voice inside your head that tells you that you shouldn't be doing this, because if you hit the glass, it could get broken, and you'll get into trouble.

Popop, my grandfather, was a tall man with a booming Austrian accent and a shock of white hair. For my seventh birthday, he introduced me to model rockets with gunpowder engines. I think he was trying to channel my instincts into something constructive and something we could enjoy doing together. I liked launching rockets and did follow the instructions at first. However, when I turned twelve, I decided to design my own model rockets composed of cardboard tubes, clay, straws, tape, and store-bought engines. Initially, I did not build them correctly, aerodynamically speaking, and in some cases the rocket would either explode or turn around and fly toward my parents and various spectators.

> A person with ADHD does not think about cause and effect, does not connect the dots between thought, action, and consequence. You shoot pebbles because you want to see them fly, and you don't think about the objects in their path.

Ironically, the dangerous mix of impulsivity and rockets came when I discovered how to make the rockets launch straight up. Then I could change their path and make them fly horizontally, oftentimes a quarter of a mile. Once my rocket went into the middle of a tennis match, and another time into a neighbor's pool during a pool party (fortunately no one was in the pool at the time). These examples are a few out of hundreds of instances of my impulsivity.

I would get an idea and be so intent upon seeing the action, experiencing the action, getting a zing from the action, that I didn't have time to think about how it might turn out or whom it could affect.

Rather than consequences, a person with ADHD thinks about the joy of seeing action. And it is this inability to make the link between thinking of an action and understanding the consequences of that action which is the definition of impulsivity: not completely thinking through the consequences of an action. In my mind, I would get an idea and be so intent upon seeing the action, experiencing the action, getting a zing from the action, that I didn't have time to think about how it might turn out or whom it could affect.

I must say that my most ingenious shooting creation was the one I called "the Crossbow," a device that I built from a building set. Originally, I built carousels and perpetual motion structures according to the instruction manual. However, I eventually became bored with the instruction manual and began to design my own devices, including cable cars that spanned the entire house, the yard, and our neighbor's yard, and yes—even things that shot. I named a fifteen-inch-long shooting device "the Crossbow" because it shared similar properties with the medieval crossbow.

My plastic crossbow was a relatively powerful mechanism that was capable of shooting an object 150 feet. I, of course, did not think of the consequences when I shot it—I simply liked to shoot it. With the crossbow, I made quarter-inch dents in the walls, I hit our first babysitter, Gloria, in the arm many times, and I made holes in some of my mother's paintings.

Many times, the crossbow was taken away from me and dismantled into hundreds of pieces. For long periods of time, my mother would take away my building set, but as soon as I got it back, I would rebuild the crossbow and then hide it in the large air vent in my room.

When I am on this impulsivity high, I almost never think, "What if?" And that is what impulsivity is all about.

solutions

The underlying question of this dilemma is how to prevent yourself from being impulsive. I suspect I will always be somewhat impulsive, but I am seventeen now, and I find I am developing more self-restraint. Here are a few ways I have found to minimize the impulsivity urge.

① **Learn from your mistakes.** The first way is simply to learn from your mistakes. This may seem counterintuitive, but I have learned a lot from these personal experiences, and hopefully you will, too, as a result of hearing about some of my stories. I rarely make the same mistake twice. I will, for example, never pour flammable liquid on a fire, shoot a crossbow near a painting, or launch a rocket near a tennis match.

② **Watch out for times when you can't concentrate.** I have discovered that my inability to concentrate triggers boredom and then impulsivity. Maintaining my concentration is very important to keeping impulsivity in check. If I can stay focused on a project or a show, I will not be bored. You can improve your concentration by being organized, identifying a task, not doing too many things at once, and taking breaks (see chapter 1).

When I cannot concentrate, I am unable to do my homework or a project, or watch a movie. As a result, I wander around the house, usually looking for something exciting to do: something active, something stimulating, something fun, or just something, anything, even if it is annoying, or foolhardy. I want to relieve the uncomfortable sensation of boredom at all costs—even if I get into trouble for doing whatever it is I end up doing.

When I do something impulsive, the action occupies my mind, and then I don't feel bored any longer—even if it means being yelled at. It is, after all, exhilarating to get attention, even if it the attention is negative. The way I figure it, anything is better than sheer boredom. So in order to avoid boredom, I'll do something impulsive. I'll tease my sister by deleting songs from her iPod account, hide my mother's diamond stud earrings while she is rushing to get dressed for a dinner out, chase the dog around the kitchen, provoke my stepfather by setting the alarm and then hiding alarm clocks where he can't find them. I do this just to get a rise out of them, but I certainly don't want to hurt anyone or damage anything. I just want to create a little old-fashioned commotion. I don't like getting punished. And I am actually sorry for what I've done, once I've thought about it.

③ **Get plenty of sleep.** You may be doubtful that sleep has anything to do with impulsivity, but it does. Controlling yourself and your impulsivity requires a lot of energy, and if you get plenty of sleep, you will have the ability to override the impulse to do something stupid (Walker 2005). I try to get nine hours of sleep a night and relax for a half hour before bedtime by watching TV or talking to my friends on IM or Facebook. Being well rested allows me to think clearly.

④ **If you have medication for ADHD, make sure you take it.** There are two reasons for this: to stop impulsive actions and to allow concentration. ADHD medicines are especially good at quelling impulsive behaviors because they allow you to think about what you are about to do and what can happen as a result of that action. It is almost as if your thought process slows down a bit so that you have a chance to understand the consequences. My medicine also allows me to concentrate. If I can concentrate, I can read *Moby Dick*, play the piano, lift weights, or watch the History Channel, and then I am not bored. If I am not bored, I am less likely to be impulsive.

⑤ **Know your own mind.** Don't let friends and others get you into trouble (Zeigler, Dendy, and Zeigler 2003). As my mother would say, "Just because someone started it doesn't mean you have to finish it." Realize that you have an inborn tendency to be impulsive, and don't let others take advantage of this weakness. Remind yourself that you have to keep impulsivity in check. Stop yourself and ask if you really want to do a particular thing. This becomes even more important as you get older and friends and other people will encourage you—or dare you—to take risks, such as doing a flip with a skateboard, going down an expert ski slope when you're not an expert, racing with a car, drinking alcohol, or experimenting with drugs. Do what is safe and right for you—don't do something that will just provide entertainment for others.

If I am not bored, then I will not be as impulsive. It's really as simple as that—and without all the fireworks.

being disorganized

the algebra final 10th grade

I sip the sweet Odwalla orange juice while studying for my final exams, all my papers spread out on the dining room table.

The soothing melodies of light classical music fill the house. It is Sunday afternoon now, and I am studying for algebra 2/precalculus. There are eight chapters, about 160 pages, to look over. I open the textbook to chapter 5, on logarithmic equations.

Netta, my brilliant and exacting Russian math teacher, expects the best from each of her students. I found math easy until I entered her algebra 2/geometry class at the beginning of freshman year, and I have had to work very hard to keep up with the class. Finally, now halfway into my sophomore year, I've adjusted to Netta's style of teaching and tests, and math is no longer a burden. I've developed a good method for studying, by redoing problems from the textbook and by taking as much space as necessary to set up the equations and calculate the problems. I glance at the rain making puddles in the lawn while I long for relief from finals. I am eating tuna with rice as I study, and I look at the seemingly infinite grains of rice and imagine all the possibilities for math problems that Netta could put on the exam.

The next morning, my mother and I hurry to meet the carpool to school.

"Okay, honey, first day of tests! Which subject is first this morning?" Mimi asks. Mimi is my nickname for my mother.

She tries to touch my shoulder, but I pull away because of my usual sensitivity to touch.

"Math."

"Oh, that should be good; you studied for five hours yesterday." Her voice is full of confidence.

"I'm just a little worried about this," I confide.

"Well, when I used to take finals, I would always get really worried and upset. Grandma would say, 'You'll do fine.' And you know what? She was right. I used to come skipping home when I got a good grade on the final."

This is a story I heard at least twelve times over the weekend.

"But these are going to be given in the strict IB format," I say. "Strict time limits. Strict formats for the calculations."

It's gray and raining. Perhaps it is a bad omen, signaling a poor grade.

We meet Kathy and her twelfth-grade son, Tony, in their navy Volvo, and I leave with them for San Francisco. During the twenty-five-minute ride, I try to convince myself to be confident because I have studied every conceivable aspect of the math. Netta will not be able to find something that I haven't studied.

"I don't like finals," I say to Kathy, quietly.

"Oh well," Kathy says in a nurturing voice, "you have to do them. Tony did them. And you'll get used to them."

Tony, who is two years older than I, says confidently, "It's all in your mind. The tests are easy; it's just logic. If you paid attention in class, you'll get it."

Tony is always very logical. Everything seems so simple for him. As a senior, he seems to have it all under control. Calm, cool, and collected, and he gets good grades. Nothing fazes him.

"I see," I say, hoping he is right.

We arrive at school and I walk into the entryway with my wet shoes squeaking on the linoleum. I look at a wet sheet of electric-pink paper for the room number for my test. When I enter the room, the look upon my classmates' faces seems worried and tired. I keep saying to myself, "I am fully prepared for this test." The supervising teacher distributes the tests.

"You may begin."

I write my name on the test booklet and open the exam. Solve: E 2X = 4. The directions near the top of the page clearly state that points will be deducted if all the calculations and all the steps are not shown on the exam sheet. The IB, or International Baccalaureate, program of study, has very strict protocols. I look at the exam sheet and look again at the directions. I search through the test looking for the space to do the work. This, I think to myself, could be a problem. I have large handwriting, and in order to do my calculations correctly, I need large amounts of scratch paper to clearly show every step. I search through the test and discover that there is relatively little workspace for each problem.

Ninety minutes later, I hand in my test to the teacher. I think the test was fair, but as I leave the room, I have an eerie feeling about its outcome.

At the end of the school day, Netta has managed, because of her diligence, to correct every test. My friends and I rush to her room, excited to find out the results. My final is handed to me, and I feel optimistic, but as I open the cover sheet, I see the C grade. I catch my breath and my heart pounds. Maybe I can't learn higher-level math. Maybe I'm not supposed to be in this school, after all. Maybe, maybe...

At the BART subway station on the way home, I put my ticket through the machine and hear a BART employee arguing with a man who attempted to pass through the gates without a ticket. I think to myself about the simplicity of their lives; they are free from the burdens of school.

When my mother picks me up at the subway station in Millbrae, the closest station to our house, I explain, "There's a problem."

Looking at the papers in my hand with the word "exam" on the cover sheet, she asks, "What happened?"

"I got a C on the math final."

There is a brief pause, followed by a sudden short intake of air by my mother. "What? You got the test back already? Are you sure about the grade?"

It continues to rain.

"I knew all the subject matter, but somehow I got it wrong," I say.

"There has to be something else wrong," she says. "You studied very hard. There is definitely something wrong."

We drive a few blocks. "I want you to look at the exam," my mother says. "I want you to figure out what happened. See where your mistakes are. That may tell us something."

At home, I scrutinize my exam. In the first problem, I squeezed my calculations into the given space. I find an error: a simple multiplication error. In another problem, I find another error: switching positive and negative signs. In a third problem, I added instead of subtracted. In a fourth, I squared instead of multiplied. It becomes clear that my exam is full of small computational errors. My formulas were correct. My approaches were correct. How could I do this? Get the hard stuff right and the simple stuff wrong? I notice that my equations were so clumped together that I couldn't follow the flow of the math. Things got mixed together.

I show my mother, and she figures out the problem immediately: disorganization. My calculations were a mess of lines and scribbles. How could I possibly think through the equations clearly? I later find out, after talking with my doctor, Dr. Bryant, that disorganization in ADHD students can show up as simple computational errors on exams. In other words, you may know how to solve the problem, but in the process of solving it, you make small errors, such as multiplying wrong or adding instead of subtracting.

cause & effect

Disorganization is a common characteristic among people with ADHD, and I've struggled with it my entire life. I have lost many things, I have a difficult time organizing my notes and books, and my handwriting has been almost illegible. I used to procrastinate and didn't know how to study correctly.

I've lost book reports, essays, and parts of important projects. One time, I even threw away half of a high school biology final because it was mixed in with some scrap paper I had used during the exam. After I left school, I realized that I had thrown half of my exam into the trash basket. I called my teacher in a panic, but almost everyone had left the school for the holiday. Fortunately, I was able to find Mr. Ulffers, the assistant principal, in his office. He searched for the exam in the trash and thankfully found it. Without the other half of the exam, I would have flunked the final.

In elementary school, my wooden desk became my home away from home. It was filled with books, old and new notepads, pieces of pencils, highlighters, erasers, dust, and, especially, papers. Papers crowded the desk to the point that, in order to do an assignment, I would need to occupy part of a neighboring classmate's desk. As a result, no one wanted to sit next to me in class. They thought that my clutter would envelop them as well. I was unable to organize my desk. It simply was beyond my ability. It made me very nervous to throw anything away, so I didn't, and the clutter just grew.

I tried to solve the problem by building storage containers, with shelves, made out of rulers, rolled up paper, and cardboard, to hold the clutter. The

> I've lost book reports, essays, and parts of important projects. One time, I even threw away half of a high school biology final because it was mixed in with some scrap paper I had used during the exam.

containers surrounded my desktop and towered two feet above me. But this was not enough, so I extended the top of my desk with more cardboard and rulers. My teachers understood that I had ADHD and let me build the towers to let me contain the clutter, and my classmates thought the towers were cool. Now, I think of what a scene it must have made in the classroom.

In fourth and fifth grades, my teachers attempted to help me solve my organization problem by giving me an extra, neighboring desk for more room, which worked until the second desk eventually became cluttered itself.

Sixth grade forced me to change my habits because of one key factor—I had to switch classes. Since I had no permanent desk and had to be mobile, I could no longer collect piles of paper. I used a binder to consolidate my papers. However, having a binder did not make me more organized. I would randomly put papers into the binder, not paying attention to the section headings, until, when it came time to hand in a report or math homework, I would have to search hurriedly through a stack of papers, dropping and scattering them on the floor. I had replaced the piles of papers on a desk with dog-eared papers stuffed into a binder.

When I moved to California in the middle of sixth grade, I decided that it was time to start fresh. I began to realize that my disorganization was hurting my grades—I was getting mere Bs and Cs when I knew I was smart enough to achieve As. I realized that in order to improve my grades, I needed to get organized. I started slowly. In seventh grade, I began using the subject sections in my binder and forced myself to place handouts and worksheets in their proper section. I happily discovered that the papers would be there when I went to look for them. As a result, the amount of work that I lost plummeted.

Seventh grade was also my first year of substantive math—meaning math that I needed to study for. I had to learn how to study properly. I began to use a notebook to take notes, because the teacher no longer handed out the notes. I realized that good study habits, along with good notes, would result in good grades on tests. I soon discovered that I am a visual learner. I remember facts by their format, pictures, and placement on a page. I decided to use this to my advantage when taking notes. In algebra, I started to use highlighters to color-code my notes. I found I could associate the color with a given fact in my notes. When I was given a test, I was better able to memorize a mathematical procedure by remembering the page on which I took the notes, the form of the notes, and then the color in which the fact was highlighted.

Multiplus!

To help even more, I created a little character whom I named Multiplus! (in the shape of an X with a neck and head at the top). Multiplus! would give constant reminders throughout my notes, further helping me to study. I used different colored highlighters for each subject.

My handwriting has never been considered neat. In fact, my mother thinks it resembles the Egyptian hieroglyphics. In elementary school, my handwriting was illegible, and teachers would ask me to resubmit handwritten papers. In fifth grade, for example, one of my words would require a height of three ruled lines. You can argue that children have poor handwriting, but with me, it was more. It was about disorganization and not caring about neatness. To solve the problem, I tried to do as much as possible on a computer, but you should realize that middle schools still tend to depend a lot on assignment handouts.

My messy handwriting, it turned out, began to affect my assignments indirectly. As late as ninth grade, I would frequently scribble an assignment down and later accidentally erase it. When the assignment was due, I would be surprised that I even had an assignment. Once, in ninth grade, I had forgotten about a geometry test because I wrote the test date in the wrong section of my binder. Luckily, a classmate of mine told me about the test during lunch, and I was able to study for twenty minutes right before the exam.

I improved my handwriting as much as I could (even though it still may not look like it), and these days I try to type as much as possible on a

My handwriting has never been considered neat. In fact, my mother thinks it resembles the Egyptian hieroglyphics.

computer. I use Microsoft Outlook to help me keep track of assignments.

In middle school, I was a constant procrastinator. The reason for procrastination is, again, not being able to organize a work schedule prior to the deadline of an assignment. In seventh grade, we had a big project known as the English Portfolio, in which we compiled our schoolwork, tests, essays, and reports, along with our analysis and reflections on our work. Even though I knew about the assignment a month prior to the due date, I left 70 percent of the work for the night before. My mother stayed up with me until 2:00 A.M., helping me to edit and assemble the portofolio, and she was not happy with me.

When I reached high school, I was assigned many analytical essays. These cannot be successfully written at two o'clock in the morning, so I had to come up with a new plan. I had to learn how to manage my time. Now when I come home from school, I finish my work before I watch TV or talk to my friends. When essays are assigned, I judge the amount of time they will take and then plan backward from the due dates. I do the majority of heavy work, such as term papers and projects, on weekends, when I am the freshest and have long stretches of uninterrupted time. I also study for tests on weekends and then review the material the night before. For final exams, I begin studying two weeks in advance and then allocate an entire weekend for finals. I have become good at managing my time and can predict the amount of time I will need to complete an assignment.

These days, I am a lot more organized than I used to be. However, I still have to work very hard at keeping disorganization under control every day. I don't like to organize my papers, and I am still very much a pack rat, but at least I don't take over a whole section of the classroom.

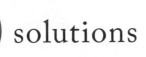
solutions

If you are anywhere near as disorganized as I was, here are some tips for keeping your disorganization under control.

① **Get help getting organized.** I did and it worked. Because you have ADHD, organizing doesn't come naturally to you. So you need to learn the *skill* of being organized. You need to learn how to plan your time and assignments. States now require that ADHD kids get additional assistance at school. There are special teachers at school who can teach you how to organize your schoolwork, notes, and studying. In middle school, I went to Ms. Melanie Love's resource class every day. During this time, she would ask me what the teachers had assigned and then show me how to plan out doing my assignments. She showed me how to take notes, how to organize my studying, and how to take the right books home for my homework and tests.

② **Organize your papers at home.** I understand that you don't have time to do this in school, but when you arrive home, there's no excuse. Set up hanging folders for each of your subjects at home, and when you arrive, put your English, math, or history papers into their separate folders. It only takes a couple of minutes. I do this every day, and so when I need to find certain handouts or notes for a test, I simply open the folder for a particular subject and easily find the papers.

③ **Start using technology.** Computers and similar devices are great for kids with ADHD. First of all, they're fun to use, and second, you are able to type (instead of handwrite), revise, and print out your assignments. Third, you can use a computer to help file and organize your papers and notes. It's the digital age: don't spend money repeatedly on binders, which you will overstuff. You can take notes on a laptop instead of taking notes by hand. Having the notes on your computer reduces your clutter factor significantly, and so you will become more organized. I have found that buying a laptop was the main way I solved my organization problem at school. But remember to back up your computer.

④ **Remember, "a place for everything and everything in its place."** I cannot tell you how many times I heard this from my stepfather, the Czar. But I have to admit he is right. If you put something back where it belongs, it will be there when you next need it. I'm always a little surprised when I put my books on their assigned shelves in the kitchen and then find them there the next morning when I'm stuffing things into my backpack for school. At the simplest level, it means developing categories for things, sorting the objects into their categories, putting the sorted objects into containers, and placing the containers in assigned spots. It also means removing objects you don't need or want (National Resource Center on ADHD 2007).

Keep your bedroom straight. If you have somewhere to put your facial creams, soaps, hair gel, cell phone, and wallet, your room will be more organized. Go to an organization store and buy plastic cases with dividers, so you have a place to put your things instead of leaving them on top of the furniture. This way, you will know where your contact lenses and glasses are—and more importantly, you'll know where the hydrogen peroxide is for your retainers and prevent it from bleaching your clothes.

Don't simply undress anywhere in your room, dropping pants and shirts all over. Have a designated area where you can undress, hang up your clean shirts and slacks, and put your dirty clothes in a hamper as you are changing. The trick is to do it immediately, because you will be more likely to do it then, rather than coming back and hanging up the clothing later. For instance, I undress in my closet and put my dirty clothes in a black hamper there. The added benefit of having a hamper is that your clothes are less likely to be stained from dirt that could be on the floor.

A little organization can do wonders for you. You may even ace your algebra exams!

being hyperactive

the T. rex preschool

The doorbell rings at about 10:30 A.M. It is Saturday, and as they do every weekend, my mother's parents—Grandma and Popop—drive north from their small town of Pelham, New York, to our house in Connecticut. Excited to see my grandparents, I run to the side door.

Since I am only three years old, I am not yet tall enough to reach the lock on the door. I pull out an improvised plastic hammer from my pocket, which I routinely use to undo all the locks in the house that are beyond my reach—including the child locks that my mother has installed on cupboards, cabinets, and closets throughout the house.

As soon as I unlock the door, Grandma and Popop push it open, and a rush of fresh April air enters the house.

"Oh, did you unlock the door yourself, my sweetheart?" Grandma asks as she kisses my cheeks. I catch a whiff of the Chester Heights Bakery crumb cake she's carrying. She brings it every Saturday.

"You unlocked the door, ha! Very smart this one is!" Popop says in his Austro-Croatian accent.

My grandmother was born in New York City, but my grandfather was born in Croatia shortly after the collapse of the Austrian Empire. He is a tall, big-boned, heavy man and has glasses and white, receding hair. My grandmother, however, has managed to keep her slender figure and always looks elegant in her blazers.

I hear my mother coming out of her room in her purple robe. Since she is nine months pregnant with my sister, her walk is relatively slow.

"Hello, hello!" she says joyfully as she approaches Grandma and Popop.

"Hi, Nadine," they say simultaneously.

"This one, here, he opened the door with a tool, you know," Popop tells my mother. His words resonate in the vaulted-ceiling living room.

"Oh, yes, I know. That's how he gets into things he's not supposed to," my mother answers.

"My little genius," my grandmother says, patting my head. There is a general giggle and then a short pause.

"So, let's think about leaving at around twelve, okay?" my mother says to my grandparents.

"Where are we going, now ?" Popop asks as he adjusts his belt. "We just got here. Do we have to go already? Don't you ever want to stay home?"

"We're going to the American Museum of Natural History in New York to look at the new dinosaur exhibit," my mother answers.

"We see dinos?" I ask in excitement.

"Yes, honey, we're going to see some dinos today!" she says as she bends over to look me in the eye.

"Yea!" I respond.

My mother, grandmother, and Popop head toward the kitchen, while I run upstairs to my room. I grab as many of my plastic toy dinosaurs as I can hold and then run back toward the kitchen, dropping several of them en route, but I make sure that my favourite dinosaur, the T. rex, does not fall.

I hear the doorbell ring again. This time it is Uncle Vinnie, my grand uncle, wearing a checked flannel shirt as usual, who has arrived just in time for coffee.

As I enter the kitchen, I smell Columbian coffee, which is brewing nearby. My mother, grandparents, and Uncle Vinnie are seated at the kitchen table, eating crumb cake, drinking coffee, and talking about Grandma's friends Mary and Eleanor. Uncle Vinnie, who loves to garden, has brought four small azaleas for my mother's garden and lined them up on the kitchen counter.

"Oh, look who's here!" Grandma says, clapping her hands as I run in.

"What have you got there?" Popop asks.

"Big dinos," I answer.

Since I can't reach the top of the table, I throw my dinosaurs on it instead, and one lands on the crumb cake. Powdered sugar puffs into the air. I climb onto the chair. My grandmother calmly retrieves the stegosaurus, now covered in sugar, and hands it back to me.

"Now it's a snow-a-saurus," Popop jokes. My mother and grandmother laugh.

"Blake, don't throw the toy in the cake," Uncle Vinnie chides. "You shouldn't do that. Nadine, teach your son not to do that."

I grab my plastic dinosaurs and begin to play.

"See, this is the T. rex," I announce, holding the T. rex in my right hand. "And this is the stegosaurus. But it's hard for T. rex to eat the stegosaurus because of his armor."

Popop, who is sitting across the table, takes the apatosaurus.

"Rawr!" he says, pretending the apatosaurus is eating the stegosaurus.

"No, that's wrong," I say. "Apatosaurus only eats plants."

"Oh, he outsmarts me!" Popop says to my mother and grandmother.

"The T. rex eats other dinos," I say.

As my mother takes another piece of crumb cake, Uncle Vinnie opens the *New York Times* and begins reading the business section. He does this every Saturday before planting new flowers.

After I've been playing for an hour with my dinosaurs, it is nearly noon and time for us to leave for the museum. The four of us get into the car, with me carrying two of the plastic dinosaurs. My mother places me in my blue car seat, buckles me in, and then sits in the front seat. My grandmother sits in the back with me while Popop drives.

"So, I heard that they have a new exhibit that just opened," my mother says.

"Really, what is it?" Popop asks.

"They have the fossil of a Tyrannosaurus rex there. The announcement was in the paper today."

"Well, we know Blake will love it," my grandmother says. She watches me as I play with my dinosaurs.

After a one-hour drive, we arrive at the museum. It's an old stone building, surrounded by gardens and blooming daffodils. As we enter the building, we discover that we're not the only ones who plan to see the T. rex fossil debut today. There is a long line of people, and, reluctantly, we have to wait.

"What's taking so long? Where's the T. rex?" I ask my mother impatiently.

"Well, honey, we just have to wait a little bit, and then we'll see it."

Since I am bored with waiting, I decide to hum the theme from *The Nutcracker* ballet. I jump, turn, and run around the other people waiting in line as the waltzes play in my head. As I look around, I see that I am not the only toddler in this museum. I am, however, the only toddler who is running around, attempting to dance to *The Nutcracker* and bumping into people. My mother tries to grab onto my jacket, but I am too excited and too fast.

After twenty minutes, and several stares and complaints about my behavior from people nearby, we are at the head of the line. My mother buys the tickets as I tug at her dress.

"Where's the T. rex?" I ask, jumping up and down.

"Okay, hold on, we have to walk to it first," she replies.

We begin to go through the museum at what seems to be a snail's pace, with Popop holding my hand. Suddenly, as we turn a corner, I see the towering skeleton of my favorite dinosaur stalking its prey. I quickly break free of my grandfather's loose grip and run toward the exhibit.

"Nadine, look, your son! There he goes!" Popop calls out to my mother.

Unrestrained, I run as fast as I can toward the T. rex exhibit, which is about forty feet away. Since she's pregnant, my mother is unable to chase me like she normally could. And Popop isn't fast enough.

I reach the exhibit, and in full view of many astonished people, I crawl under the rope, over the small wall, and onto the hardened clay base of the display. I am standing next to the dinosaur and reach up and touch the T. rex's leg. I look up at the massive four-foot-long jaws. A monster.

Within seconds, all the alarms go off, resonating throughout the hall. Lights flash. The crowd parts as the security guards run toward me and climb into the exhibit. When my mother finally catches up with me, two security guards hand me over to her. A technician then turns off the alarm.

"Ma'am, you must keep your child out of the exhibit! This fossil here cost the museum millions," one of the security guards says in a Southern accent. The other guards are frowning at her, shaking their heads.

As I look around, I see that I am not the only toddler in this museum. I am, however, the only toddler who is running around, attempting to dance to *The Nutcracker* and bumping into people.

"Did you see how out of control that child is?" asks a bystander. "I blame the mother. No discipline."

My grandmother is holding her head and hiding her eyes as she always does when I do something wrong. She's trying to be invisible.

"I'm sorry, sir. I didn't realize he would take off," my mother says. "He broke away from us, and I can't keep up with him."

"You must control your child," another guard says flatly, "or we'll have to ask you to leave the museum."

Popop drops his head to talk to me, trying to look inconspicuous but considering his broad, 6-foot 1-inch frame, that is impossible.

For the remainder of our stay, as we tour the other exhibits, two security guards follow my mother, my grandparents, and me. I don't understand why they have to keep watching me; we aren't near the T. rex anymore. Popop grasps my hand more firmly.

But I am satisfied. I have accomplished what I came here to do: I have touched a real T. rex.

cause & effect

I have always been hyperactive. Extremely hyperactive. In fact, my mother told people for years that I didn't just run around the house, I flew around. Despite her own seemingly boundless energy, she sometimes admits that I am the only one in the world who can exhaust her.

In the T. rex incident, I was infatuated with dinosaurs and eager to touch bones that were sixty-five million years old. Nothing was going to stop me. My curiosity and energy compelled me to get through the security fencing to touch the dinosaur bones. It was one of the most memorable days of my childhood, but now I think about what could have happened if I had toppled a sixty-five-million-year-old treasure. Not a good thing.

In fact, I've found that my sometimes-overwhelming curiosity and energy lead to a lot of hyperactivity. If I am curious about a certain subject, I will put all of my efforts into understanding it and pursuing it. This amount of energy is enormous, hard to contain, and hard to control. One counselor, George Lynn describes ADHD kids as being "like tigers in a zoo who may feel an enormous amount of pent-up energy, but may be distressingly unable to focus it or control it." He goes on to say that in order to reduce the pressure, ADHD kids may "provoke people around them, but it doesn't come from malice, but from a need to bring attention" (Alexander-Roberts 1995, 7-8).

On a typical day at home, when I was younger, I would wake up at 5:00 A.M. I would be ready to build towers with my K'nex blocks; bake cupcakes in the kitchen when I wasn't supposed to be baking; chase Ashley and Becky, our two springer spaniels, up and down the long hallway and around the kitchen island; read a Thomas the Tank Engine book; play a Treasure Island computer game; watch TV; race Matchbox cars; or construct a fort in the backyard out of plywood and gardening tools I found in the garage.

Once when my grandmother was babysitting and I was in my building mode, she made the mistake of leaving me alone while she answered the phone. Within ten minutes, I had emptied the large hall closet, pulling out all the sheets, comforters, and towels, and constructed an entire fabric village in the family room for my sister and me. It took my grandmother over an hour to clean up all the linens, and I was sent to my room for a long time-out.

If I am curious about a certain subject, I will put all of my efforts into understanding it and pursuing it. This amount of energy is enormous, hard to contain, and hard to control.

When I became interested in chemistry at the age of eight, I would mix baking soda and vinegar in a closed water bottle and then wait until it exploded all over the kitchen from the pressure. Early on Sunday mornings, when my exhausted parents would try to sleep in, I would make volcanoes, which erupted in a gooey foam all over the kitchen floor. I rushed into doing these things without any self-control and without considering any of the consequences of these experiments, because I wanted to do them and I wanted to be busy. Again, with ADHD, you feel compelled to reduce the pressure of the energy you have, without any regard for the mess it will create—and without any thought of taking an experiment outside so it doesn't explode in the kitchen, coating all the walls, which then need to be cleaned.

My mother worked long hours at her high-tech corporate job during much of my childhood. When I was eight years old, she brought my father and me to a skyscraper in New York for a rehearsal for a major IBM press conference announcing a new line of mainframe computers. My mother thought it would be good if I could see her work and meet her coworkers. While the executives were rehearsing their speeches in the darkened meeting room and the videos were playing on the big screens, I took advantage of the commotion to sneak away from my father and climbed into the back of the big mainframe demonstration computer that was being featured. The computer was fascinating. Suddenly, an IBM director saw me and went running to find my mother while other people coaxed me out of the computer. "Nadine! You have to get your son out of the back of the computer. It's not safe for him, and he could bring the entire system down! We may lose the computer demo for the national press conference!" Needless to say, I didn't bring down the computer, and the Monday morning conference went on as scheduled. But I never again was invited to a press conference rehearsal.

These are all examples of my hyperactivity. I must always fully occupy myself. The truth is, I love stirring things up, too—even if it means getting into trouble. At first, it may seem counterintuitive to cause trouble, since punishments will result. But I have found that I have a voracious appetite for attention—whether positive or negative—and hyperactivity is a means by which I obtain this attention. I don't provoke to be bad, but from the need to release the energy and get the attention. As I've grown older, I've learned to channel my hyperactivity in more positive directions.

solutions

Hyperactivity is part of ADHD. To keep from getting into trouble, you can either channel it into something constructive or unleash it in a controlled situation.

① **Channel your energy into something constructive.** If you are hyperactive and have a seemingly infinite amount of energy, you can channel that energy into accomplishing something. For instance, you could construct a doghouse, complete a homework assignment, play guitar, join a club, do sports, ride a bicycle, do exercise, or just walk the dog.

Community service work is also another excellent way to channel your energy constructively into something beyond yourself. Find a cause you are passionate about, a cause that needs visibility and that may not be popular, and pour your energy (and your heart) into it!

I became passionate about greyhound rescue work when my family adopted our first greyhound, Odette, a regal, fawn-colored, five-year-old, from an Arizona racetrack. She was in a group of dogs that had been flown in by rescue volunteers in small private planes in a program called Wings for Greyhounds. I soon learned that thousands of these young and loving dogs are killed nationwide each year (10,000 in 2006; Greyhound Protection League 2007) if they are not adopted after they are released from racing. Susan Netboy, founder of Greyhound Protection League, a national non-profit greyhound advocacy organization, has been monitoring the greyhound racing industry for twenty years. Netboy states: "Documented evidence confirms that greyhounds have been killed by shooting, electrocution, starvation, sale for medical research, and lethal injection. In addition, large numbers of greyhound puppies that don't show a talent for racing are destroyed on the breeding farms. But through the hard work of dedicated rescue organizations, an increasing number of greyhounds have been adopted in recent years." I became passionate about doing all I could for the rescue effort. I went with my family and other greyhound families and our dogs to fairs, set up information booths, and talked to hundreds of people about greyhound adoption. I worked with Petco in San Mateo, California on greyhound adoption days and at fund-raisers. Service work like this can be all-consuming, which is a good thing. You are preoccupied doing work for others.

Another way to channel your energy is to become involved in music. Classical music, in particular, is very good because I believe it is both relaxing and complex. Because it is highly mathematical, it is very soothing to the mind. Oftentimes, in the middle of my homework, I will go to the piano to play a Chopin étude or Mozart piano sonata. If I am nervous, I suddenly find that I can relax and my mind seems to be better able to focus. My piano teacher, Tony Ignatius, who is a concert pianist, believes that classical music develops the mind. He recently told me about the findings of a doctor at MIT, Dr. Nadine Gaab, who has shown that musical training helps certain brain functions (Gaab 2006). I just know that I find classical music soothing, and I believe that playing it helps me to think more clearly.

② **Unleash your energy in a controlled situation.** When you have too much energy and no task to complete or occupy your time, you need to find a safe way to drain your energy. You could do a sport, like running or swimming, or something highly creative, like building or painting. When you are older, you can try archery and golf. Anything that involves a lot of concentration is good.

③ **Take your meds.** Again, ADHD medicines can help a lot. Without my medicine, I feel aimless, like a tiger in a cage. I have an enormous amount of energy, but I can't focus it, and I can't seem to accomplish anything. Once you have decided what activities you want to pursue, the medicines can help you channel your energy into those activities.

I realize that I have a boundless supply of energy and that it has to be released somehow. But I also realize that I have a choice. And so do you. All you have to do is learn how to channel your energy in a positive direction, like getting a good grade on a school paper rather than pursuing a dinosaur!

having tics

the roman conquest of carthage

6th grade

Sixth grade. History class. Thirty minutes until lunch. I'm beginning my presentation about the Roman conquest of Carthage. About two minutes into the presentation, I feel a tic coming. I attempt to repress it, but my effort is useless. I jerk my neck backward and then forward. The whole class stares at me. I rub the back of my neck to pretend that I am just relieving neck pain, and my attempt to cover up the tic works; the students in my class look away, having dismissed the possibility that there is really something wrong with me, that the tic is a sign of some mental condition.

However, a minute later, I'm on the verge of another tic. I'm talking faster about the Carthaginian general Hannibal and the elephants he used in battle. The tic is coming. Now, I'm talking about the Roman catapult and how the Romans could build such an engineering marvel in the field of battle. The tic happens, and the class stares at me a second time, but they stare more thoroughly this time, as if thinking, "We did see something very odd," and now they watch to see if it will happen again. I rub the back of my neck again, and I "cover" the tic. But a minute later, I have another tic. I rub the back of my neck again, but I'm not convincing anyone this time.

My social studies teacher, Ms. Lea Wedge Morrison, looks at me with a concerned expression, and when I make eye contact with her, she interrupts my presentation and says, "Blake, are you okay?" She is a beautiful blonde with sparkling eyes who makes history exciting for us.

I answer, "Oh, yes, my neck is just bothering me."

I look at my classmates, who are now scrutinizing my every movement. I'm finished with my presentation. And they will never regard me the same way again.

My family and I have just moved in the middle of sixth grade from a little town in Weston, Connecticut, to a suburb of San Francisco. I have wanted so much to make a good impression on my new classmates. I wanted them to like my presentation and, therefore, to like me. Now, they will think of me as odd—and as one of the ones to be dismissed. I feel defeated—just like Hannibal.

cause & effect

The incident in sixth grade was just one of many situations I've lived through as I have struggled over and over again with a tic condition, which often can accompany ADHD. Some young people with ADHD also have tics.

In fact, scientists have found that two-thirds of children with ADHD have at least one other coexisting condition (Biederman, Faraoue, and Lapey 1992). Simple tics and Tourette's syndrome seem to commonly occur with ADHD (Adesman 2003).

Simple tics are sudden, repetitive, involuntary movements or sounds. They can include such behaviors as eye blinking, mouth opening, sniffing, throat clearing, or head movements. Usually, simple tics are temporary; they come and go and last for less than a year. Suddenly they disappear, but they can change and reappear again at a later time (National Resource Center on ADHD 2007).

Tourette's syndrome is a little different. It is a condition that includes vocal tics along with motor tics; both vocal and motor tics have to last for more than one year for the condition to be diagnosed as Tourette's (National Resource Center on ADHD 2007). Vocal tics include throat clearing, coughing, barking, or repeating words or phrases; they may also include screaming and saying some bad words. Motor tics can range from simple movements like eye blinking, lip licking, grimacing, or mouth opening, to more complex movements, like head jerking or shoulder shrugging. Tourette's syndrome is usually mild, and it is often accompanied by other conditions—ADHD being the most likely. Sixty percent of children with Tourette's also have ADHD (Barkley 1998). The main difference between simple tics and Tourette's is that with simple tics, the tics come and go. With Tourette's, tics persist; they don't go away.

My doctors believe that I have a simple tic disorder that is chronic, meaning that a tic will appear at certain times, especially when I am nervous, and then disappear. The tic changes and comes back, only to disappear again. As far as I know, my tics first appeared when I was very young. Over time, they became stronger and stronger, and to counteract them, my doctor gave me clonidine, a blood pressure medicine, to take along with the stimulant medications I was taking for ADHD. The clonidine worked for a while, but my doctor had to keep increasing the dosage to help neutralize the tics. When a new medication for ADHD—Strattera—was introduced, my doctor switched me to that, and the tics lessened considerably and almost disappeared. I say "almost," because tics have reappeared during stressful times, whether it was moving, changing schools, meeting new people, taking final exams, or interviewing for high schools. Tics also can occur when you are tired.

I, myself, have had several kinds of tics—and I must admit that some of them were quite bizarre. When I was in third grade, I had a motion tic in which I had to twirl in a circle. This twirling created an imaginary spiral of bricks around me, and every time I twirled, another layer of bricks was added. I twirled in one direction, but then I was obligated to twirl in the other direction in order to feel balanced. If I did not complete the cycle four times, my mind did not seem satisfied. Eventually, after four cycles, I found I would become dizzy and would be forced to stop.

In fifth grade, I had a rather unusual tic—banging my chest and making a noise while I did it, almost like Tarzan. But I wasn't trying to be like Tarzan. I did it because I felt a shaking in my lung when this tic occurred. After completing the cycle of the tic, I would feel better and could continue with whatever I was doing at the time.

In seventh grade, I had a vocal tic in which I continued to repeat "101." This is the highway number of the Bayshore Freeway leading to San Francisco. Something about the rhythm of the words captured me, and the tic started. There was comfort in repeating and making the numbers resonate: "1...0...1 (Hey!) 1...0...1."

Another, more recent tic occurred in ninth grade. This tic was more sedate and more common looking—blinking. I would blink my eyes repeatedly to feel the pressure of my eyelid against my eye until the tic was satisfied.

The basic fact about tics is that I am actually reluctant to have them. Yet even though these tics persist, my mind never seems completely satisfied. When one tic ends, there may be nothing for a while. And then suddenly, another one begins.

> The basic fact about tics is that I am actually reluctant to have them. Yet even though these tics persist, my mind never seems completely satisfied.

I have minimal control over which tic will come next, and it usually is a total surprise.

Tics are not conscious, yet they are not totally unconscious. They are, instead, something in between.

My mother often pleads with me to stop the tics. "Blake, can you control this?" she asks. "Blake, can you stop this? Please don't do this. People are looking at you. People will wonder why you are doing that."

And she doesn't like the answer I give her. I say, "I can—and I can't—control the tics."

"What do you mean, you can and you can't? Either you can or you can't." She becomes exasperated.

I cannot tell you how many hundreds of times we've had this same discussion. The reason is that tics do not occur entirely by themselves. I consciously make the effort to move whichever muscle is needed to execute the tic. However, this conscious effort is driven by an unconscious inclination, almost a warning or a signal, that a tic is on the way. I think about how I will feel if I were to turn in a circle, or repeat certain words, and then, unable to resist, I allow the tic to happen.

solutions

The underlying question of tics is how to stop them. I have found a number of methods. Hopefully one of these methods may help you if you are bothered by tics.

1. **Force yourself to stop the tic.** It may seem rather obvious, but it is actually possible to stop tics or, at least, to delay and decrease their occurrence. Before a tic happens, you need to consciously stop the associated muscle from moving. That is, you need to try to override the impulse to allow a tic to occur. Although you will probably end up with the tic anyway, it's important to postpone it, because postponing the tic will aid in preventing another tic from occurring,

and ultimately aid in ending the tic altogether. Another idea is to do a different movement that competes with and helps neutralize the tic. You can do this competing movement for three minutes after the tic occurs and each time you sense that a tic is about to occur (Woods, Miltenberger, and Lumley 1996).

Again, when a tic is finally subdued or defeated, a different tic will probably develop eventually. It is something you may just have to live with. Sometimes it may be possible to conceal the tic by making it seem like something else. For instance, when I had the blinking tic my excuse was that my contact lenses were causing eye irritation. Some vocal tics can be concealed with coughing, which is seen as something normal and natural.

② **Focus on something else.** Another method to help end a particular tic is to focus your mind on something else, on something entirely different. For instance, I have found that exercising, such as swimming, running, or weightlifting, helps to relax me. Being calm and focused on something else reduces the frequency of tics.

③ **Try meditating.** If the methods described above are not successful, you can also try meditating. Many times, tics can be caused by stress, and meditation can reduce stress. Meditating is usually associated with yoga and sitting with your legs crossed, but this is not the only way to do it. I have found that simply walking slowly in a quiet, rather picturesque Mother Nature-type scene lowers stress and therefore helps to stop tics. Researchers at the University of Illinois Urbana-Champaign found that "children who spent a few hours after school or on the weekend playing outside in green natural settings showed a significant reduction of ADHD symptoms" (Kuo and Faber Taylor 2004).

④ **Get your rest.** Being tired can bring on tics (National Resource Center on ADHD 2007), so get plenty of sleep. I routinely try to get nine hours of sleep a night. It helps with the ADHD, and it helps reduce tics.

⑤ **Check the dosage of the medication you're using.** In some young people, the frequency of tics can also be intensified by higher dosages of medications you take for ADHD (Pliszka, Carlson, and Swanson 1999). So you may want to look at your dosage, altering your medication or combining your medication with clonidine, which treats mild tic disorders.

I took stimulant medications for ten years: from the time I was five years old until I was fourteen years old. The medications were great and helped me to concentrate and focus, but my tics became progressively worse, and I had to take clonidine in response. But, as always, there was a catch: if I were to suddenly stop taking the clonidine, whether it was my own forgetfulness or if I had simply used up the pills, my blood pressure could suddenly drop and then rocket back up. Clonidine needs to be taken consistently.

One time, when we were away on a weekend vacation and forgot my clonidine pills, my parents pleaded with three different local pharmacies late at night to give me two pills for the weekend so that my blood pressure wouldn't plummet. This was a stressful experience. The very pill that was supposed to relax me had the exact opposite effect. Talk about being upset. My parents went from pharmacy to pharmacy. Meanwhile, I was wondering what was going to happen to me if my blood pressure dropped. Would I faint? Would I have to go to the hospital?

When I switched to taking Strattera (a nonstimulant medication) for my ADHD, I was able to focus, the tics decreased, and we no longer had panic trips to the pharmacy late at night.

⑥ Tic talk. Another method to eliminate tics is, believe it or not, to talk about them. Tell your classmates and friends that you have ADHD. Tell them that you also have tics.

It is annoying and embarrassing to have a tic in the presence of other people. Your family, like mine, will be accustomed to whichever tics you may have, and so there is little awkwardness in the at-home situation. As my sister Madison once said, "Why are you talking about ticking all the time? What are you, a clock?" But nevertheless, talking helps defuse the tics.

When you meet an adult, perhaps a friend of your parents, and you have a tic in front of them, they will be cordial and pretend that you never had a tic. If tics occur at school, though, it is likely that you could develop a reputation as being eccentric, as I did when I was presenting the report about the Romans and Carthage and as I did before, in earlier grades. So, the only way to really deal with this is to tell people. Tell them you have ADHD, and tell them sometimes tics go along with it and that they should just ignore the tics. Your friends will be able to question you about your tics, and if they are true and reliable friends, they will understand your condition. When a tic happens, say, "Oh, there it goes again," and dismiss it, and keep on talking or doing whatever it is you are doing. You'll find that other people will dismiss it too. I also found that once you tell people you have tics, you are less likely to have a tic in their presence, for you are no longer trying to cover anything up. You are removing all the stress from the situation. And a lot of what tics are about is nervousness.

⑦ Know you have lots of company. As a last resort, always remember this: Doctors say that lots of kids have tics— tics occur in up to 20 percent of all children. If you consider that tic disorders occur in 0.3 percent of the general population of the United States, that equals about nine hundred thousand people who will have tics some of the time (American

Psychiatric Association 2000). So tics are far from rare. They are actually quite commonplace. Knowing that fact can really help.

I've struggled all my life with tics, and they did get the best of me for a while, but they haven't defeated me. Maybe I'm not like Hannibal after all.

— 6 —

being unpopular

my best friend Aki 5th grade

"Hiya!" I call out as I throw the snowball at my best friend, Aki, and watch delightedly as it hits his arm. I fix the buttons on my navy winter jacket to protect myself from the cold air of December. It's fifth grade in Connecticut.

"I'm going to get you, Blake. This is war!" he laughs. He throws more snowballs at me, but I dodge them.

"You missed. You'll never get me!" I shout. But there's no response from Aki behind his snow fortress near the edge of the road. I suspect a trick, so I stay in my fort on the front lawn. After a few minutes, I begin to wonder what has happened.

"Aki, you there? Come and face it like a man!" I call. I briefly search the snow-covered lawn and then inhale a breath of frigid but fresh winter air. Anticipating a surprise attack, I begin to make more snowballs.

I have just made the second snowball when Aki suddenly appears on the left side of my fortress and pelts a snowball at my face. I'm wearing goggles to protect me. I take a huge snowball and blast it into his nose.

"Oh god, that's cold," he shouts.

I laugh as I hear the rumble of a snowplow coming up the hill to remove the blizzard's fourteen inches of snow from the road.

"The snow thing is coming," I say. "Let's go." As I get up, I see Aki struggling to move.

"What's the problem?" I ask.

"My foot is, like, stuck."

The rumbling snowplow enters the cul-de-sac in front of my house.

"Aki, it's coming. We have to go."

"But my foot is stuck."

"Okay, let me help you."

I pull Aki by the arm, but in doing so, I get stuck in the snow as well.

"I'm stuck too. " I start waving my arms as the snowplow approaches.

"Blake, it's coming," says Aki.

We wave our hands furiously, but the old bearded driver inside doesn't see us. The window of snowplow cab is fogged over. The snowplow is chewing up the snow within feet of us.

"Nooooo…" I say.

Suddenly, Aki and I are engulfed in a huge, white four-foot-high wave of snow as the snowplow passes us, just narrowly missing us with its blade and wheels. We begin to laugh uncontrollably.

"Well, that was fun." I clear the snow from my face.

"Oh, I can move my foot now," Aki says.

"I think that's the closest I'll ever get to being in an avalanche," I say as we walk toward my house, our feet sinking deeply into the snow with every step. The sky is darkening.

We enter my house. Our sitter Gloria is sweeping the snow away from the doorway. "You two go outside and brush off now!" she says, eyeing all the snow on our jackets. She doesn't want to have to clean up an area that she has just swept. We brush off the snow and remove what seems like infinite layers of turtleneck sweaters and jackets. Snowball fights are worth it, though.

Aki stays for dinner. Before Aki, I rarely had a friend come over to my house. It was hard for me to make friends. At school, kids avoided me and teased me. So, in response, I started isolating myself from them. In fact, during lunchtime, instead of eating with the rest of the kids at the long tables and playing kick ball outside, I would go to the library and read encyclopedias. My books became my only friends.

One day after class, Aki came with me to the library, and we read together. The following day, we read together again and then talked about what we had learned. After two weeks of reading together, I summoned up enough courage to ask Aki over to my house to play. Aki was a lot like me, except he didn't have ADHD. When we didn't visit each other, I called him every night to talk about the planets, Galileo, or currency exchange rates. I was so happy to have found one good friend. And I invested all of my time and energy in him. Having one friend was an accomplishment for an ADHD kid like me.

After having hot chocolate, Aki and I go up to my room. I leap onto my bed, knocking the Thomas the Tank Engine pillow out of the way. Aki sits on the futon beside my bed.

His face suddenly lights up with an idea. "You know, we should go play laser tag sometime!"

"That would be so fun," I say. I'm happy that he's offering an idea for a future playdate. My eye blinks with a tic, but he pretends not to notice, and I'm thankful for that.

"I think the minimum number of players needed is six," Aki says.

"Oh, but I don't really know that many people that I could ask," I respond, somewhat embarrassed by the fact that I don't have any other friends.

"No worries, I'll invite some of my other friends," he says.

I am elated. I will be part of a group. "Aki, that sounds great."

I am so happy about the invitation that I want to show Aki one of my inventions. "Do you want to see this new thing I invented out of a building set?" I ask. I want to show Aki that I am smart and creative and therefore worthy of his friendship.

"Sure."

I go into my closet where I keep the crossbow that I have just designed and built from my K'nex building set. I load the crossbow in the dark and then quickly open the door.

"Bam." The rubber band snaps against the back of the crossbow and shoots the K'nex projectile. It hits Aki's arm.

"Oww! That stings," Aki cries.

My heart starts pounding. I didn't mean for it to hit Aki. I was so anxious to show him how my invention worked that I didn't think it could fire accidentally and hit him. As usual, I hadn't thought of this possibility.

"Aki, are you okay?"

"Blake, why did you hit me?" Aki asks, puzzled and a little hurt.

"Aki, I'm sorry. I didn't mean for it to go off. The crossbow just misfired."

"Let me see that," he says, recovering from the sting. "This is cool. You invented this? You didn't use instructions?"

"It's all my invention," I say with pride. I think to myself, "He is a good friend."

"We could have an excellent war game with this," he says.

Having a best friend is like a badge of honor. It's saying to all the kids at school that I am worthy. I finally feel normal and accepted. Someone besides my parents actually likes me! Aki is someone who can put up with all my faults—my physical awkwardness, my bumping into people, my silly antics, my getting up and down from my seat continually, my tics, and even the lion sounds that I sometimes make to cover the tics—because he is able to see beyond all of these behaviors and appreciate my other qualities. He just looks the other way when something doesn't go right. It never occurs to me that anything can go wrong in a friendship that is so effortless.

My mother, however, notices that I have just one friend. She worries that there could be an argument or disagreement and that the friendship could abruptly end. She encourages me to make other friends, but I don't know how to make other friends. I protest that Aki is the only friend I want or need. We enjoy talking to each other and building inventions. Why do I need other friends?

At the end of December, our fifth-grade teacher, Mrs. Motroni, plans a weeklong gingerbread-house-building class. Parents bring in Tootsie Rolls, candy canes, and lollipops to supplement the basic gingerbread houses. For the first time in a while, I am actually excited about going to school.

"I want to build a skyscraper like those in Manhattan," I say to Aki. Holiday music plays in the background.

"Well, let's hope that it stands up," he says. "I don't think gingerbread is supposed to support that much weight."

I pause a moment, listening to the music and thinking about how to support a gingerbread skyscraper. "I have an idea," I say. "I can use the long part of candy canes as support," and I go off to get some candy canes.

The sweets are displayed on buffet tables, not far from Aki's desk in the classroom. As I walk away, I catch a glimpse of Jack, a friend of Aki's whom I dislike, leaning over in his chair to talk to Aki. As I pretend to count candy canes, I carefully listen to the barely audible conversation between Aki and Jack.

"Aki, why are you friends with Blake? He's so different. He blinks his eyes, makes noises, and weird stuff like that."

"I don't know," Aki responds.

I wait for Aki to say something in my defense.

"Well, if you're friends with him, that makes you look bad too, you know," says Jack.

There is silence as Aki thinks about this.

"And then, if you're friends with him," Jack adds maliciously, "and I'm friends with you, that'll make me look bad, too."

"Well, I guess he is a little odd," Aki admits.

"A little odd," I think. Did Aki say that? He didn't say anything about our discussions, our inventions, how I help him with math homework. I delay collecting candy canes in order to hear the rest of the conversation.

"Exactly," Jack says. "So don't be friends with him. Our popularity is at stake."

Jack pushes his seat into its original position and continues to build his gingerbread house. Knowing that the conversation is over, I return to my seat with a fake smile, concealing the fact that I've heard the conversation. My stomach hurts.

"Well, I got the candy canes," I say anxiously to Aki, as I start blinking with a tic. But Aki does not respond, and instead he glances at me with a questioning expression, as if assessing me all over again. He stares at his gingerbread house. From this moment, things start changing between us.

My tenth birthday is in May. I decide that I want to have my party at the Discovery Museum, where we can take a simulated space shuttle flight. My father leans against the kitchen counter while eating a lose-weight-fast Jenny Craig breakfast and reading the *New York Post*. My mother sits down with me at the kitchen table and drinks her daily dose of coffee. She looks up at me.

"Blake, we'll need ten children for the simulated space shuttle flight," she says.

I think about how I can come up with ten friends to invite.

Later that day in class, I tell my three desk mates the news.

"Oh really?" Danny replies, interested.

"Sounds cool," says Ryan enthusiastically.

I am encouraged. The initial responses are good.

"Oh," Aki interjects. His response is lukewarm. "Do you think it will be fun?" he asks, as if to reassure himself that his time at my party will not be wasted.

Aki comes to my house later that day. When my father walks into the kitchen, our two springer spaniels, Ashley and Becky, swarm over him. My father holds out space shuttle party invitations.

"Aki," I say, "look at these! Aren't they great?"

Aki smiles weakly.

"My birthday party is in just twenty more days," I say.

"That's nice. So when are we having dinner?" he asks, looking at the clock. His question seems out of place.

"I don't know, maybe in a half an hour or so." As I answer his question, Aki looks at the clock again. He seems anxious for the playdate to end. There is silence as I think of something to say.

"Well, I hope you can come, because you're my best friend," I say.

"I should be able to," he says. His answer is not as definite as I'd like it to be.

The next Sunday morning, my mother sets up a workstation—with pens, stamps, rulers, envelopes, and the letters—on the kitchen table where she and I will endure the tedious task of addressing invitations.

"So, who are you going to invite?" my mother asks as she sips her coffee. "Are you making friends with other boys?"

"Well, I invited some other kids."

"That's good. You need to have other friends. Everything you do shouldn't just be with Aki, Aki, Aki." She repeats his name to make a point.

I notice the birds outside are chirping in an annoying, repetitive tone.

"I'm just saying, don't put all your expectations into one friendship," she adds. "It's like putting all your eggs in one basket."

I dismiss her comment, thinking that I don't really need to make more friends. If I have one good friend, mission accomplished.

On the morning of the party, my mother says, "I'm so happy we have enough kids to fill all the positions on the crew." She goes through the hour-by-hour schedule for the party.

Suddenly the phone rings, and it's Ryan.

I hold my breath, thinking, "He is going to say he can't come."

"I'm getting a ride with Danny's mom to your party, but she says we might be fifteen to twenty minutes late, if that's all right," Ryan says. "Oh, and Luke will be with us, too."

I let out my breath, relieved.

"We'll definitely make the space shuttle flight, that's certain," he replies. He seems eager to come to my party and frustrated by the twenty-minute delay.

During the morning, we get several more calls from my friends' parents, mainly asking for directions. It is 10:20 A.M., now, and my mother and Gloria are packing the plastic treat bags, filling them with lollipops, Tootsie Rolls, and chocolate. I am watching a television program on hurricanes.

My father walks down the hallway into the living room. "Are you ready to go, Blake?"

The phone rings again.

"Oh, you gotta be kidding me! All morning, this phone!" My father pauses as he opens the car door. "Just don't get it. Let's go. It's already eleven fifteen."

It is Aki. Anticipating his question, I answer, "The museum is on the right side of Park Avenue off of Interstate 95. It's on the Bridgeport-Fairfield line."

"Well, actually, I was not calling about that. I was calling because I can't come to your birthday party." His response seems simple and mechanical.

"What happened? Are you sick?"

"No, it's just that I have a baseball game."

I think he's joking, and I wait for him to say, "Just kidding," but instead there is a pause.

"It's my tenth birthday party," I say. "It's a special birthday. We have the shuttle flight!"

In the background, my father shouts from the garage, "Blake, come on. We have to go."

"No. I can't come," Aki replies.

"But you knew about this party for a while!"

I imagine his mother standing in the background, telling him what to say. I want to end the phone call.

"Good-bye," he says.

Suddenly, I understand. This isn't just an ordinary good-bye. He is saying he doesn't want to be my friend any longer.

"Who was it?" my father asks as he backs the car out of the garage.

"Aki," I respond.

"Don't these people have maps? It's like they've never driven to Bridgeport before."

"No, it wasn't that... He said he couldn't come."

"What? Why not?" My father turns on the air conditioning.

"Because of a baseball game." I look out of the car window.

"Well, that's a stupid reason."

"I know," I say, "and now that I think of it, he didn't even apologize or say he was sorry."

"Well, then, I guess he's not such a good friend."

Such a good friend, I think. He's my only real friend. I don't feel like talking the whole way to the museum.

When we enter the Discovery Museum, the others have already arrived. Danny, Luke, and Ryan, as it turns out, managed to arrive on time.

"Happy birthday, Blake!"

I smile as my classmates surround me. No one asks where Aki is.

cause & effect

The fact that I had really lost my best friend hit me later that evening, after the wrapping paper had been cleared from the floor and the leftover birthday cake placed in the refrigerator. I was numb. How could Aki do this to me? Suddenly, I was alone again, without a best friend. At school, Danny, Ryan, and Luke remained friendly to me. They said hello to me and even asked me to sit with them at lunch sometimes. But I was mostly on my own again, going to the library at lunch and sitting with my books. It took me a long time to get over the way Aki had treated me.

Everyone wants to have friends, but making friends is hard for kids with ADHD. Throughout the first nine or so years of school, I was so insecure about my ADHD that I had a hard time making friends. I was afraid that my ADHD behaviors would get in the way, and they did. I

I was so insecure about my ADHD that I had a hard time making friends. I was afraid that my ADHD behaviors would get in the way, and they did.

often bumped into people without realizing it and without saying, "Excuse me." Sometimes, I would get so excited about what I was talking about that I'd wave my arms and accidentally swat someone. Other times, I would interrupt people when they were talking and start asking questions about something entirely different from the conversation underway.

I didn't have the natural instinct that most people have to notice and understand nonverbal cues, like when someone frowned or looked annoyed or confused, or whether they were bored by what I was saying. People often thought I was being rude or inconsiderate. My sister called me "clueless." I was the person who didn't get the joke when everyone else did. On top of all that, I sometimes had sound tics. In order to cover up the sound tics, I would make another noise—a cough, a sneeze, or a goose or lion sound. I wanted to be seen as being silly—but that backfired and made things worse.

Throughout elementary school and part of middle school, I was teased for all my ADHD behaviors, which didn't help me make any friends. I was regarded as different, and kids don't want to be friends with someone who seems unusual. They fear it will reflect badly on them—as Aki feared. When you meet new people, it is within the first thirty seconds that they decide whether they like you or not. If you behave somewhat differently, then they can easily decide not to become friends with you. I probably gave the impression that I did not want friends, which was not at all the case.

This is not to say that I didn't have any friends during elementary or middle school. After Aki, I became good friends with Danny, Luke, and Ryan. We launched rockets together, built towers, and went Halloween trick-or-treating together. We became a group in sixth grade, but then my family moved away, and I had to start all over again. And it wasn't easy. I think some of my other friends were friendly to me because they figured out that I could help them with their homework. Others thought I was funny in a bizarre sort of way.

Approaching friends was hard work for me, and it did not come naturally. I didn't know how to "schmooze," as my sister would say. For example, if I wanted to invite a friend over, I would call that person up and say, "Hey, this is Blake, do you want to come over?" They would often just say no, because they were caught off guard. I had to learn how to chat and then work up to an invitation.

Since I was nervous about calling friends on the phone, my mother came up with a solution. Before making a call, my mother and sister would have me write down exactly what I wanted to say to my friend: "Hello, this is Blake. What did you think of class today? Chat, chat, chat." I would rehearse the script with them, and then I would call my friend and ask him to come over and play. I had to learn this skill like I was learning a new subject in school. I tried to create a science of how to make friends. And it worked.

Another thing I had to learn was how to approach a group of kids. I used to send my sister, who is three years younger, into the group to break the ice. Once she was able to enter the group, I'd follow her and be immediately allowed in because she had paved the way. Then again, this only worked when she was around. On other occasions, I would summon up my courage to approach a group, walk up, or actually barge in, and then expect everyone in the group to start talking to me. Of course, they didn't, and instead would move away from me. My worst fear was realized, which only made it harder to approach a group the next time. Eventually, I learned how to wait along the perimeter of a group, make eye contact, smile, and receive a smile in response (a signal of acceptance) before entering.

My mother was right about the importance of having more than one friend. It's better to have a few friends so that you are not going to one person all the time. If you rely on the friendship too heavily, your friend will either feel suffocated by too much attention or get bored with doing things with you all the time. Believe me, I know from experience.

I also learned a lesson about fair-weather friends. Some people will not appreciate your qualities; you have to find those who do.

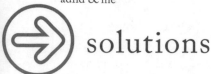 # solutions

Just because you have ADHD doesn't mean you have to go friendless. However, you may need to learn how to make friends, as I have. I have become—not to boast—well liked in school, and so can you. I've found that there are several keys to being liked.

You need to know that if you want to have friends, you need to like yourself first. After that, you need to know that people appreciate others who have good social skills. If you don't have good social skills, you will be rejected. People with ADHD tend not to have good social skills because of three ADHD symptoms—not paying attention, impulsivity, and hyperactivity (National Resource Center on ADHD 2007). And that is where all the problems come from. But if you learn how to work around these symptoms, you'll be able to make friends. Here are some of my solutions.

(1) **Make friends with yourself.** It's important that you like yourself if you want others to like you. You may be thinking, how can I be likable—ADHD and all? Well, in case you're wondering, the last chapter of this book (chapter 15) is all about the great qualities you have—and you have many.

(2) **Learn to pay attention.** Not paying attention means you miss important information during a conversation. You want to pay close attention to people's reactions—their body language, their expressions, their tone of voice, the look in their eyes. Notice their choice of words to better understand the real meaning of what they're saying. Notice any actions that might be revealing what their real feelings are. I found a book on body language that helped me understand these hidden clues. Also, you can use the "echo technique," in which you paraphrase, or put into your own words, the key idea that someone has just told you to make sure that you heard what he or she said (National Resource Center on ADHD 2007). Remember, too, that if you make a promise to someone—for example, if you promise to

IM the name of a song—you follow through and do it. People like it when you do what you say you will do. It shows that you keep your commitments. It shows respect.

③ **Don't put your foot in your mouth.** You need to control your impulsivity. Don't interrupt when others are speaking. First, you won't hear what they are saying, and second, you will upset them, because they will think that you are not interested in what they are saying. They will think you are self-centered or rude. Don't speak or act without thinking about what you are saying and how it may affect the feelings of the other person. If you have an opinion about someone, don't just blurt it out. Count to ten. Slow down and try to be nice (National Resource Center on ADHD 2007). Maybe a good rule to follow is don't say something if you can't be nice.

My mother put me into a social skills group. In it, I learned how to call up a friend and schmooze, how to pay attention to what other kids were saying so I could respond appropriately, how to enter a group, how to wait my turn, how to avoid interrupting (even when I was feeling very enthusiastic), how to avoid being rude, and how to avoid being restless and appearing uninterested. You can also role-play with your family to practice these skills.

④ **Stop tapping your foot.** Being hyperactive means fidgeting, which makes it look like you aren't interested in listening to the other person. If you are fidgeting while attending a concert, class, religious ceremony, or other event, it may seem that you are anxious to leave and may appear disrespectful when you're not trying to be. Hyperactivity also can make you overly talkative, so try to slow down, because you don't want to be seen as a motormouth. Being talkative can be annoying if you don't give others a chance to talk. Again, other people will think you are being overbearing and are uninterested in them or their thoughts. Be considerate.

(5) **Learn how to shake hands.** Etiquette class, was, again, my mother's idea, and at first I thought it was a colossal waste of time. I joined the class in middle school, and I learned how to introduce myself, converse with others, approach a buffet table, tie a tie, and dine at a formal dinner. I refused to dance with girls, however, and purposely went to the end of the boy's line, knowing there were fewer girls than boys in class, so that when we were matched up, there would be no dancing partner for me. Unfortunately, I outsmarted myself, and I ended up having to dance with Mrs. Millet, our teacher! But etiquette class helped me to improve my personal image. I realized that having good manners made me more likeable to other kids, and grown-ups even began to compliment me on my manners. Knowing what to do can give you confidence, whether it's how to enter a room, how to approach people, or which fork to use.

(6) **Let go of insincere friends.** So-called friends who do not respect you do not deserve your friendship. Aki initially was a good friend because he enjoyed our discussions, snow fights, and trips to the library. But then he proved not to be such a true friend. When he changed his mind about my party at the last minute without any concern for me or for my parents and the elaborate arrangements they had made, I learned that he was only a true friend when it had benefited him. Realize that there are insincere people out there, and their insincerity is not a reflection on you. You may have to be alone for a while until you find new friends, but don't worry, you will find them.

So, ADHD symptoms can sometimes get in the way of making friends, but you can learn how to work around your symptoms. And despair not. You will find many people out there who are worthy of your friendship.

being bullied

the tape recorder 6th grade

After waking up with a sore back from sleeping on a futon, I open my suit-case and put on a clean shirt and a pair of cargo pants. Looking outside, I see it's pouring down rain. I think, "It's still better than the December black ice back in Connecticut." My family has just moved to Northern California, and the moving truck hasn't yet arrived. We have little furni-ture in the house, and I don't even have a regular bed to sleep in yet. I am eleven years old, in the middle of sixth grade. It's Monday morning, and this is my first day at my new school.

Like any newcomer, I dread being the new kid on the block. But I'm especially anxious because I have ADHD, and I'm afraid it's going to show up in front of my new classmates.

After my mother and I go to the school office to fill out the paperwork, I am brought to English, my first class. The teacher, Mr. Mackenzie, looks up from his desk and smiles at me.

"Okay everyone, be quiet for a second. This is our new student, Blake Taylor."

He manages to draw all the attention to me, creating an embarrassing situation. All eyes scrutinize me, and then a general "hello" echoes throughout the classroom.

The desks are clustered together in groups of four to allow students to interact. I sit with two girls and a boy named Brian.

"Hi," I greet my table partners, as I accidentally knock my notebook and loose-leaf binder off the desk. The anxiety and nervousness of being new is at its greatest. Although my classmates watch me with confounded eyes, they don't yet know me well enough to either ask or ridicule me about the reason for my awkwardness. I have that advantage for now. Eventually, I will tell some classmates that I have ADHD, as a means of explaining my awkward behaviors.

Over the next month, Brian becomes my first friend. I learn about how he can build remote-controlled cars from scratch, fly gas-powered model airplanes, and repair sprinklers. His zeal for constructing things, however, has won him the reputation of being a nerd.

In February, Mr. Mackenzie rearranges the table assignments, as he does every two months, and Brian and I are moved to a table next to a boy named Phillip. Phillip has the typical Irish features: red curly hair, freckles, and green eyes.

"Today, we will begin our poetry unit," says Mr. Mackenzie.

"What should I write about?" I ask Brian happily. I've started to feel comfortable in my class.

"I don't know. A car?" he suggests.

"Oh, how about a snake? Yeah, that's what I'll do." I start scribbling down words in my large handwriting, which resembles scratches on a page.

I push my elbows out to balance myself on the desktop, and books and colored pencils spill onto the floor.

"I'd be surprised if you can write a poem about anything while dropping everything and making a scene," Phillip interjects slyly.

Brian and I exchange looks, trying to understand the reason for this verbal attack.

"Is something wrong?" I ask Phillip.

He doesn't bother answering, but instead looks over at Brian and then back toward me.

"You know, your friend here," he says, pointing at Brian, "is the weirdest nerd I've ever seen."

Apparently, Brian and Phillip have known each other since elementary school.

"Just shut up, Phillip," Brian replies.

Before Phillip can think of another mean comment, Mr. Mackenzie announces that poetry time has ended. We won't have to suffer any more of Phillip's insults for the time being. However, we have eight more weeks of this seating arrangement and, therefore, eight more weeks of having to endure Phillip.

With time, Phillip's comments become increasingly frequent and spiteful.

Phillip turns toward Brian. "So, have you made any new friends lately?" he taunts. Brian doesn't respond and instead looks down at the desk in dismay.

"Oh, that's right," Phillip sarcastically answers his own question as he looks into the air pretending to be thinking, "You can't make any friends. You'd rather fix cars and sprinklers."

Brian seems helpless.

"And I'm sure you would make friends with the way you talk," I reply.

"Like you would know, shake-boy." Phillip begins to taunt me by jerking his head around in imitation of my tic. "Hey look, I'm Blake. I can't stop shaking my head." He is the only one laughing at his joke.

I adjust my glasses, readying myself for battle. "Seems like everyone's laughing," I answer. We are fighting a war of sarcasm.

"Just leave us alone, Phillip," Brian says.

"You're so stupid," Phillip says to Brian. I find this comment ironic considering Brian's engineering abilities.

Before the argument can escalate any further, English class is thankfully over.

The faculty at Crocker Middle School pride themselves on helping to resolve differences between students. For a public school, the behavior rules are unusually strict, and therefore the slightest hint of harassment—whether physical or verbal—is not tolerated, provided that the teachers see or hear of the infractions. Fights seldom break out in school. The strict detention system, which will penalize you for chewing a piece of gum, threatens harsh consequences for those who even think about starting a fight.

As a result, undercover verbal harassment is the weapon of choice among middle school students. And this harassment is common, because, unlike a physical fight, where there is ample evidence, like cuts and bruises, spoken words simply vanish into the air without a trace. Phillip is keenly aware of how to circumvent the school's disciplinary policy, knowing that no one can obtain proof of his mean-spirited language—or so he thinks.

After more than three weeks of verbal attacks, I ask Brian, "So what do you want to do about Phillip?" I take a bite of my turkey sandwich.

"I don't know. He's a real jerk," says Brian.

"If we, like, tell Mr. Mackenzie, I guess, we would be tattletales, and that would be humiliating," I say.

"Your reputation would be ruined," Brian says. "And Phillip would make fun of us about that, too."

Undercover verbal harassment is the weapon of choice among middle school students. And unlike a physical fight, where there is ample evidence, like cuts and bruises, spoken words simply vanish into the air without a trace.

"We can't fight him," I add, "because then we'll be blamed, even though he's the one who started it."

I tell myself that there has to be a way to outsmart him. I get an idea and decide to run it by my mother after school. I have been talking to her about the Phillip ordeal ever since it began, and we've been strategizing about how to defuse his comments. For instance, we have discussed handling his comments using a combination of humor, answering back, and ignoring him. I can tell that my mother is troubled, worried about me fitting in. I make her promise that she will let me handle the situation, because I do not want her contacting Phillip's parents and ultimately ruining my reputation at school.

"I want to record Phillip on a tape recorder," I say.

My mother takes a thoughtful breath. "Okay..."

We go upstairs to her office, and after searching for a few minutes through the desk drawers, we find her miniature black tape recorder. Now, I need to find a place to hide the tape recorder, a spot where Phillip will not see it but where it will still be close enough to record his insults. After thinking for a minute, I decide that my nylon pencil case, attached to the inside of my binder, is the ideal place to house the tape recorder. I prepare to collect evidence the next day.

"Today, we're finally going to get Phillip," I say to Brian the next morning. I describe how I'm going to use the tape recorder.

"Oh, that's cool; let's do it!" Brian smiles widely, feeling relieved, liberated, and excited all at the same time.

Brian and I go to our table, followed by Phillip. I put my binder on top of the table and stick my hand inside the black pencil case where the tape recorder is sitting. I put my index finger on the record button and press it down:

"*So, have you been shaking your head lately?*" Phillip asks slyly.

The first piece of evidence is gathered. Brian almost starts laughing.

"*You're so stupid, you can't even answer a question,*" Phillip says to me. Then to Brian, he chides, "*What are you laughing about, nerd?*"

Brian attempts to draw Phillip out more. *"Hey Blake, I built this really cool remote-control car."*

"Yeah, that's all you do, fiddle with cars, and that's why you have no friends," Phillip responds. *"You, too, Blake. You don't have friends either. You're not popular. And you don't dress the right way."*

The tape recorder is getting all of this. I am amazed my plan is working so well and that I'm letting Phillip provide his own words to incriminate himself.

"This English class is so stupid," Phillip begins again. *"I have more important things to do than sit here with the two of you—one a nerd, the other an ADHD case."* He is baiting us, but we don't respond, and, luckily, he keeps on talking.

"I have a lot of friends, and I have a lot of fun with my friends. We do cool stuff, like burning things. We burn lots of things, and we don't get caught. You know, I have a life." Phillip prattles on.

I almost open my mouth in shock, hearing that Phillip is not only a bully but also an amateur arsonist. But I restrain myself, hoping he'll keep going. Phillip is doing a beautiful job of providing evidence.

"Well, I don't enjoy destroying property," I answer.

"Well, that's your problem." Phillip happily uses my response as a springboard for an insult. *"You don't do anything that's fun. And you shake your head. You're always dropping things and bumping into people. That's why no one likes you."*

I put my pencil case away. I don't want to risk having Phillip find the tape recorder. After English class, Brian and I play back the tape, and to our relief, Phillip's voice is loud and clear. When I return home, I play the recording for my mother, and we agree that the next step is for us to go to the school principal, Mrs. Chun. We ask Brian and his mother to join us.

I think to myself, "I can defeat the bully and still preserve my reputation at school." I am not, after all, being a tattletale. I am just the messenger. Phillip has provided all the words. My classmates will view me as intelligent and courageous for bringing this bully to light.

"So, what's been going on?" Mrs. Chun asks when she meets with us.

"Well," my mother begins, "one of the students, named Phillip, has been harassing Blake and Brian on a daily basis for the past five weeks."

"Yes, I've heard the same from Brian," says Brian's mom.

"What does he say to you?" Mrs. Chun asks me.

"Well," I say, as I reach into my backpack to pull out the tape recorder, "he says a lot of things. And some of his comments are recorded here."

Mrs. Chun looks with amazement at the tape recorder.

"Very cunning," says Brian's mother.

I put the tape recorder on Mrs. Chun's desk and rewind the tape to the beginning. Phillip's words spill out:

"You're so stupid, you can't even answer a question.... Yeah, that's all you do...and that's why you have no friends.... I have a lot of friends.... We burn lots of things, and we don't get caught."

After she's heard the recording, Mrs. Chun responds, "Well, your case is very strong." It's more serious than she had initially thought. "I'll talk to Phillip and his parents about this," she says.

The next day, Phillip is gone from school. In fact, he is gone for three days. It is actually pleasant in English class for the first time in weeks.

When he returns, he looks sullen. His eyes are downcast, and he avoids looking at Brian and me. He is no longer on the offensive. He is humiliated, knowing that he was outsmarted in a very public way. Outside of English class, Phillip approaches me.

"Blake, I'm sorry I was such a jerk. I picked on you because of your problem. I was also jealous of you. Jealous of your grades and that you could do better than me in school."

I am taken aback by Phillip's plain honesty in facing me. I am silent.

"It's okay," I finally respond. There is nothing more to say. Phillip had insulted me because of my ADHD, but in the end, he's been forced to respect me—ADHD and all.

cause & effect

In every school, there is a strict and brutal caste system. There are the kids who belong to what is often called the "popular group" and all the rest, who are not part of that group. Many of these kids will form their own smaller groups, which are often referred to as the "other groups" to distinguish them from the one and only "popular group." And then there are those kids who dwell in the gray area between all the groups, hoping and waiting for acceptance and entry into one of them. The kids with behavioral and physical differences typically dwell in this gray area. If you have ADHD, like myself, you may not be good at reading other people's expressions, you may not wait your turn, you may blurt out answers in class before others can answer, or you may climb around and pull things away from others—all of which may isolate you from your classmates. Kids with ADHD are also easy prey for bullies.

I tried to explain to my classmates that I couldn't help many of my awkward behaviors. I became the class clown to try to cover up these things, but that didn't stop the bullying. Bullies noticed that I would accidentally bump into people on the lunch line or spill my milk on their sneakers, be impatient, and spread out my papers and books and gadgets all over my desktop, oftentimes oblivious to my desk partner. These bullies would ridicule me when I had tics. Once they decided that I was unusual because of my ADHD mannerisms, they had a base from which they could launch an attack and criticize me on everything else.

When I was younger, they criticized nearly every aspect of me—my appearance, my personality, my intelligence (even though I got good grades), and my ideas. If I created something unique such as an art project or came up with a bright idea, they would do their best to destroy it or put it down. Since I could not keep constant guard over my creations, I had to devise countermeasures to protect them. I used intelligence and cleverness to solve the bully problem. And you can do this too, if you work at it.

In elementary school, I enjoyed constructing mailboxes and other paper structures on my desk, and my classmate enemies seemed to get great plea-

sure in knocking them down. In response, I rein-
forced my paper mailbox and desktop structures
with rulers and pencils. I would sharpen pencils
and hide them in the paper structures so that if a
bully hit one of them, he would be jabbed with the
pointed tip.

> I used intelligence and cleverness to solve my bully problem. And you can do this too, if you work at it.

In sixth grade, I built two five-foot perpetual
motion towers out of K'nex building sets to dem-
onstrate principles of physics to my science class.
Classmates who disliked me because of my ADHD
would try to kick the towers when no one was
looking, to knock them down. I then designed and embedded crossbows
into the structure, which would be triggered if someone kicked at the
towers. Just knowing that the crossbows were there proved to be a deter-
rent for bullies.

I gained some notoriety for protecting my things during the 2004 pres-
idential campaign, when I was a high school sophomore. Being one of a
handful of Republicans at my San Francisco school, I posted Bush-Cheney
stickers on my locker. Some of my classmates defaced my campaign stickers with graffiti or peeled the stickers off of my locker. To try to stop this, I
glued the stickers to my locker and covered them with plastic wrap so that
it would be difficult to write over them in pen. Still, my classmates continued to mark up my stickers.

Next, I went to the drugstore and bought two vibration-detector alarms
that would go off if anyone tried to disturb my stickers. I put the alarms
under paper to conceal them, and then superglued them to my locker.

Unfortunately, I didn't think about the possibility of vibrations coming
from other sources. When a classmate slammed his neighboring locker
door shut, the alarms, which were several times louder than an alarm clock,
both went off. Ms. Rissman-Joyce, the principal of my high school, whose
office was just down the hall, ran out of her office. Teachers and students
from nearby classrooms surged into the hall. My math teacher, Netta, ran
out of our precalculus classroom and pried the alarms off of my locker. She

returned and handed the alarms to me in front of the entire class and said I would be hearing from the principal.

As it turned out, after I pleaded my case, the principal determined that I was just exercising my right of free speech and that I had the right to protect my campaign stickers. I didn't get into trouble for using the alarms, but I was counseled about how they were easily triggered by all kinds of vibrations and told that I needed to remove them.

Later that year, my art teacher selected my papier-mâché egret sculpture for display in the main high school hallway. Since I had spent twenty-five hours creating and molding the six-foot sculpture, I was determined to protect it. I decided to use motion detector alarms this time, which were triggered by light, to protect my art. Unfortunately, again, the alarms went off by accident, triggered this time by the shadows of students as they criss-crossed the hall. My French teacher thought that it was a fire alarm and had all of us evacuate our classroom. This time, I did get in trouble and was told never to bring alarms to school again. (I should mention, however, that since then, no one has ever bothered my locker or any of my artworks.)

Generally speaking, bullies are people who are either insecure in their own life or jealous of yours. Throughout elementary school and part of middle school, it seemed that the bullies I faced were jealous of my intelligence or creativity and the fact that I was different. (You may be realizing that you, like many ADHD kids, are intelligent, creative, and different too.) Whenever I would present a project or complete an assignment, they would attempt to belittle either my work or me. Bullies fear someone who does better than them because they fear the competition. But then, bullies will also attack you if the opposite is true—if you get bad grades. For instance, receiving a C or D on a history paper gives bullies license to criticize you and say that you are stupid and will never achieve your goals in life. Another thing bullies may attack you on is your physical appearance. If you are sloppy, heavier, or poorly dressed, you are providing bullies with yet

> Generally speaking, bullies are people who are either insecure in their own life or jealous of yours.

another way to criticize you. They may, for example, make fun of your nose, eyes, short height, greasy hair, or unfashionable clothing. Basically, bullies must find a scapegoat—someone to tease and disparage—in order to improve or secure their own social standing.

solutions

How you react the first time you meet a bully often determines how that person will treat you from then on. Different strategies work better in different situations. I've had some success with all of the techniques described below. Teachers, parents, and counselors recommend some of them, and I've added a few of my own.

① **Use humor.** Using humor is a good technique because it helps defuse the bully and the situation. The bully wants a confrontation, and bringing humor into the situation can neutralize the tension. It shows the bully that you have a sense of humor and can laugh at yourself and your faults—which is not something the bully wants. The bully wants to inflict pain. So, the next time a bully says, "You're stupid," agree with him. You could say, "Yeah, I'm having a really rough day. The brain cells aren't working."

② **Answer back.** Using sarcastic remarks can be an effective weapon, and I have found that sarcasm can, at times, shock or silence a bully. Say to a bully, "Oh, really?" in an amazed, exasperated tone. Or say, "Who cares?" or "Thanks for noticing" (Borba 2006). Realize, though, that your remarks can also have the opposite effect and easily anger someone and inflame the situation.

③ **Avoid the bully.** Avoiding a bully is an option, but many times it simply just buys you time, because eventually you and the bully will confront one another. Avoidance does, however, provide a solution when you are unprepared, not having the right comebacks ready, to face a bully.

④ **Call them on it.** Showing strength in the face of a bully is good. You want to show that you will stand up to him or her. Stand up straight, hold your head up confidently, and look the bully directly in the eye. Ask the bully, "Why did you say that? Are you trying to be sarcastic? Are you trying to say you don't like me because I am tall/short/blue-eyed/black-eyed…?" (Borba 2006). This may succeed in deflecting the bully, who is always a coward and looking for easy prey. Don't make it easy for the bully to attack you, and he or she may leave you alone simply because bothering you is not worth the effort. Fighting, of course, is not an option, because you will both get into trouble and could be expelled from school. Bullies, like anyone else, do not like it when their intentions backfire.

⑤ **Use positive self-talk.** Whenever you feel that a bully's comments are getting to you—that you are actually starting to doubt yourself—remind yourself of your accomplishments in life. Think to yourself: "I beat those guys during that tennis match." Or, "I achieved an A on my math exam!" Or, "I have a friend who really likes me for who I am." This is called positive self-talk. Boost your self-esteem and think logically. Remember that bullies are afraid and insecure, and they try to destroy your self-confidence so that they can feel more powerful. They fear someone who could be a competitor, or someone who is intelligent, kind, or different. Bullies put other people down, or taunt them, because doing so makes them feel bigger and better. They hope that the other kids, the bystanders, will look up to them and fear them. Fear plays a big part in all of this.

(6) Get help from adults. Reporting someone to a teacher or parent is generally considered by kids to be tattling—the kind of thing you do in elementary school. But reporting a bully is not; it is entirely different. When a bully purposely harasses you, he or she is trying to cause pain by hurting you or embarrassing you physically or emotionally. It is abuse and you need to report the harassment to stop the abusive behavior.

This kind of behavior is not tolerated in the adult world, so why should it be tolerated in middle school or high school? Get your facts together—times, places, dates, what was said, witnesses who heard the comments—and seek an authority figure. Ask a really cool teacher for help. If kids accuse you of being immature, realize you are actually being very mature in how you are handling the situation. If kids accuse you of not being able to solve your own personal situations, guess what? Bullying is tough, and they're right. It's not something you can solve on your own. You generally do need assistance in solving it.

My mother helped me a lot. When I would come home from school each day, she and I would discuss the situation with Phillip and devise ways to solve the problem. We would discuss comebacks to his comments. One day, she told me just to ignore him. Another day, when he was criticizing my clothes, she said, "Give him the facts. Tell him you shop at the Gap, the same place everyone else does. So, what's the problem?" Another day, she said, "Use humor with him. Make a little fun of your odd habits."

So, we discussed the Phillip problem, and, in doing so, it made it seem like less of a problem. First, I understood from my mother that what Phillip was doing was not right. Second, I didn't feel isolated. We were a team, trying to figure out what to do, and it was just a matter of finding the right technique to fix the problem—which, of course, was the tape recorder. It was important to have this moral support from my mother. At the very end, we called in Mrs. Chun, the middle school principal, to help us, and she recognized the situation for what it was—harassment—which she was not going to tolerate in her school.

However, I will add one piece of advice. Only report a person when the bullying is out of hand. Don't report someone every time your feelings are hurt. Your classmates will think you are babyish and unable to handle your own problems, which, ironically, may increase the bullying, because you are giving the bully another reason to ridicule you. On the other hand, if you are uncertain about handling a situation by yourself, talk to a parent, teacher, or another cool adult. They've probably been through this and can offer good advice.

Sometimes, you may find yourself uncertain of whether you should confide in an adult or keep it to yourself. In this case, you can talk to a trusted friend. As you progress through middle school and high school, your friends and you will grow in maturity and be better able to think through problems. A trusted friend may be able to give an adult answer without being an adult. Furthermore, this friend will be more familiar with the details of the social order in your school than any adult and may be able to give you some important insight.

Remember, the best solution is to use words. Stand your ground and use words against bullies. Interject something funny to defuse a bully, or call them on their mean comments and actions. Question their intent in front of everyone. Use words to plead your case to the school administration. Use your natural intelligence and wit. Oh, and tape recorders are good, too, though you may want to skip motion detectors and vibration alarms!

being isolated

the first dance 6th grade

The alarm clock wakes me up at 7:40 A.M. As I brush my teeth, I happily think about how it is not only Friday but also only one week until summer vacation. After putting on a T-shirt and cargo pants, I go into the kitchen.

"Hey, honey," my mother greets me, placing a grilled cheese sandwich for me on the table.

My stepfather, Ben, whom I refer to as the Czar, clomps in. On the wooden and marble floors, his boat shoes make the sound of a galloping horse that can be heard throughout the house.

"Hi Blakester," he says, clearing his throat.

"Hi." I bite into the grilled cheese.

My stepfather turns to my mother. "Nadine, do you want to tell him about tonight?"

"Okay," she says. "Blake, there's a middle school dance tonight…"

"I know. I'm not going," I quickly interrupt. I fix my glasses nervously, afraid of what she might suggest.

"… and we want you to go," she concludes.

"But I don't want to." I can hear my voice rising. I am thinking, "How can I go? How can I face all my classmates at a dance?" The second half of sixth grade at my new school has been a difficult semester for me. I haven't made a lot of friends to make up for the ones I left behind in Connecticut, and I am still adjusting to being in a new place. Also, sixth grade has had its share of teasing and put-downs. Why would I want to go to a dance?

"Look, it'll be fun. You get to dance with girls," my stepfather interjects, as if this were something I was worried about.

"So? I just don't *want* to go, okay?" I'm getting close to yelling. I envision myself standing in clear sight of everyone else, exposed and scrutinized, just like in science class when everyone was selecting lab partners and I was left until last. I don't have the self-confidence to endure it.

"Well, you're going," my mother states flatly.

"No, I'm *not*," I reply. "I can make my own decisions."

"Okay, I'll make a deal with you," my stepfather says, offering a compromise. "If you go to the dance, I'll take you out of PE class this afternoon."

There is a long pause during which the only sound is the incessant birds chattering outside. At this point in my life, I have an utter aversion to PE class. Because I feel awkward, I hate running the required mile, and I don't want my classmates to see me come in last, or nearly last, when we run it. The thought of skipping a two-hour PE class and ending school earlier is appealing.

"Okay, fine, but you have to pick me up from the dance after one hour," I reply.

"How long is the dance?" my stepfather asks.

"It starts at seven and ends at nine thirty."

"Okay, how about I'll pick you up at nine o'clock?"

"No, eight," I negotiate.

"Okay, eight thirty then."

"Okay, deal."

We shake hands, and I leave with my mother for school.

"Do I really have to go to this stupid dance?" I ask her as we get in the car.

"Look, honey, don't exclude yourself from your classmates. Get involved. You'll have fun."

"Yeah, sure," I reply sarcastically. "Fun."

Four hours later, it is lunchtime, and I go to the school library. As I used to do in Connecticut, I tend to stay by myself at lunchtime. It is easier to retreat into my weather and geography books than to listen to the gossip about who is hanging out with whom, who went to someone's home or party, who told the teacher on someone. God knows what they are probably saying about me.

My parents' alibi for my leaving school early is that I have a dentist appointment. As we leave, I feel relieved that I don't have to suffer through PE. But, nonetheless, this escape has come with a price—going to the school dance.

At home again, I play the computer game Red Alert while my sister, Madison, watches TV. Over time, we have developed the uncanny ability to split our attention among television, IM, and computer games. Before long, it is six o'clock, and the dance is imminent.

"Okay, Blake, we're going to leave in forty-five minutes," my stepfather announces.

I start to get anxious. My heart starts thumping. I am keenly aware that dreading the dance isn't helping the situation. I have to find a solution to survive the impending one-and-a-half-hour ordeal. I decide that I will bring something with me that I can hide in my cargo pants. They have large side pockets capable of carrying and hiding relatively large loads. My mother has refused to buy me a Game Boy, so that is not an option.

I am keenly aware that dreading the dance isn't helping the situation. I have to find a solution to survive the impending one-and-a-half-hour ordeal.

However, I could bring a book. The side pockets of the cargo pants cannot, obviously, hold a big encyclopedia or atlas (my favorite forms of literature). But if I can find a book small enough, I can slip it inside. I go to the bookshelf and find one, *The Pocket Encyclopedia of Insects*. I slip the book in my right pants pocket and zip it so it's not visible. I am now prepared for the dance!

My stepfather approaches from his room with his galloping boat shoes.

"Okay, ready to go?" he asks as he puts on his tan leather jacket.

"Yes," I reply reluctantly, unconsciously tapping the encyclopedia in my pocket.

As we back out of the driveway, he lectures me on common dance etiquette.

"Now if a girl asks you to dance, you always have to say yes."

"But what if I don't want to dance?"

"Well, you can't hurt her feelings."

I stuff eleven pieces of cinnamon gum in my mouth to try to calm my nerves.

As we approach the auditorium where the dance is being held, the sunlight has already faded. My stepfather drops me off in front of the building, where my classmates are clustered in groups. All heads turn as I exit the car. I feel that they are looking at me, analyzing me. I start to twitch. As I approach my peers, I announce, "I hate this!"

There is general laughter among the classmates who have heard my complaint.

"Then why did you come?" one of them inquires, snickering.

"My stepfather made me."

"Oh, ha, ha," the others laugh, further confirming my fear that I will be ostracized once inside the auditorium.

The doors open, and all the other kids flood inside. I am the last one to go in. The music is pop and hip-hop. The incandescent lights, in every color from blue to red to yellow, irritate my eyes in a way that they don't affect other people. I am very sensitive to bright lights, touch, and loud sounds. It comes from ADHD. As soon as everyone is on the dance floor, I hide behind a folded-up lunch table and pull out the antidote to my anxiety: *The Pocket Encyclopedia of Insects*. It is relatively dark inside, even near the door, but the strobe lights create barely enough light to read the book. I open it to a page labeled "Bombardier Beetles." I try my best to ignore the beat of the music and to hide myself from my classmates.

I only manage to read the first paragraph before I run into trouble. A girl sees me behind the lunch table and decides to approach me.

"Hey, Blake, do you want to dance?" She assumes I want to dance because I am, in fact, at the dance.

I know well that I am not supposed to refuse her request, but this is a desperate situation for me: I have to survive an hour and a half without being dragged out onto the dance floor, where my classmates will look at me and make fun of me.

"No, I don't want to dance. It's okay," I say, violating the first rule of my stepfather's etiquette lesson. I start to say that I was forced to come to the dance by my parents but find it too complicated to explain over the music and the flashing lights.

It's too dark to see her facial expression, which is perhaps a benefit. She walks away. Within a mere three or four minutes, a male classmate approaches me.

"Hey, dude, you want to come and dance with the group of us over there?"

"No, thanks." I disobey yet another rule of etiquette. I am turning my back on guy friends. This is not turning out to be a good evening.

"All right." His tone of voice insinuates, "You're only hurting yourself."

I have already isolated myself this year, and I've spent most of my lunches and free time away from other classmates. I'm worried that if I dance, I will be subjected to stares and comments. I'm afraid that I won't be accepted for who I am. Being afraid of not being accepted keeps me from going out there to begin with. I'm afraid that if one of

I'm afraid that I won't be accepted for who I am. Being afraid of not being accepted keeps me from going out there to begin with.

> I realize that I have miscalculated the problem of the dance. I am frantic that too many girls are asking me to dance.

my ADHD behaviors comes out, then everyone on the dance floor will label me as eccentric or bizarre. In effect, I isolate myself preemptively.

Subsequently, another girl asks me to dance. More girls come up to me, and I refuse them, one by one. They are becoming a nuisance. I realize that I have miscalculated the problem of the dance. I am frantic that too many girls are asking me to dance. It's time to change my tactics.

Considering that my house is well within walking distance, I decide to try to escape into the night. But there's a hitch. Teachers monitor all the entrances and exits. If I succeed in getting out and someone notices I'm gone, they will call my mother. Knowing my mother's protective nature, our town's police force will be on alert within minutes. So I have to come up with an excuse before leaving.

"Where are you going?" a teacher inquires.

"I'm just going to get a drink of water."

"Okay, let's go together."

I discover that the school requires teachers to escort students whenever they leave the room. My escape plan has been foiled. I reenter the auditorium reluctantly and begin to read the insect book again. A teacher sees me reading the book and alerts the other teachers to my self-imposed isolation. It is just my luck that they figure I need some help to get involved in the dance, and they send another girl over to ask me to dance. This probably explains some of the kids coming over to me earlier.

"Blake, let's dance."

"No, thanks," I reply, wondering how many times I have to reread the same paragraph.

"Come on, just one dance."

"No, I hate being here."

She shakes her head.

A male friend of hers attempts to pull me onto the dance floor, but I resist. During a break from this incessant pestering, I look at the time on my cell phone. It is, thankfully, eight fifteen. I call home.

"Hello," my stepfather answers.

"Ben, please, you have to come pick me up now."

"But it's only eight fifteen."

"Yes, I know, you said eight thirty, so I'm reminding you." It's difficult to talk over the loud and jarring music.

"Well, I don't know if I can pick you up at eight thirty."

"What? But you said!"

"I know, but your mother wants you to stay there longer."

"Stay longer? Please put her on then."

"She's in the shower."

"This is absolutely ridiculous!" I am incensed.

Part of the compromise—that I will be at the dance until no later than eight thirty—they've decided to ignore.

"Fine, bye!" I snap closed the clamshell cell phone. I have to face yet another hour of torture. At nine fifteen, my stepfather finally arrives. I jump into the front seat of the car and slam the door.

"It's about time!" I cry. I am so shaken by the dance that I begin to tremble. I make my best effort to hide my tears.

"Blake, what happened?" He is distressed and doesn't move the car.

"What do you think? I hated it. Please move the car."

"Oh, come on, Blake. Did any girls ask you to dance?" he asks, worried that no one has asked me to dance or join in.

"Too many. Completely ridiculous." As I exit the car at home, I take the insect book out of my pocket.

"You took a book!" he says with a combination of shock and laughter.

"Yeah, that's right!" I jog downstairs to my room and close the door. Through the floorboards, I can hear my stepfather say to my mother upstairs, "Nadine, he took a book."

"A what?" she answers in disbelief.

"A small insect book or something. He said too many girls asked him to dance."

"Oh god." I imagine her putting her hand over her mouth.

I hear my mother's footsteps, along with the horse-galloping ones of my stepfather, descending the stairs. My mother opens the door to my room.

"Honey, what happened?"

"The girls asked too many times. Now leave me alone!" I start to cry.

"Oh, come on, that's good that they asked you." She tries to hug me, but I push her away.

The ticking clock in the background fills the awkward pause.

"I hated it. Okay?"

"Well, I would have loved to have your problem when I was your age," my stepfather jokes.

"Okay, that's good for you then." How can he understand what the real problem is? I am being exposed, humiliated, and picked apart by my class-mates. How could I trust them to become my friends, only to be rejected because of my ADHD habits and behaviors?

"Honey, we just want you to try it, just once," my mother says. "I'm sorry that we pushed you too far."

My mother and Ben leave the room, and I fall asleep quickly. I am relieved that the ordeal is over. As it turns out, I don't return to another dance for two years, until the last dance at middle school—the eighth-grade graduation dance—one that I end up enjoying. I danced every dance with girls. Dancing is now, believe it or not, one of my favorite things to do.

cause & effect

For some people, my experience at the sixth-grade dance would seem good; classmates were asking me to join in, and many girls were asking me to dance. But I did not feel flattered like most kids would. Instead, I felt awkward, shy, and intensely apprehensive. I feared, either rightly or wrongly, that if I were to join the crowd, I would be ridiculed and ultimately rejected.

I have always been shy, or so my mother says. Of course, I don't think of myself as shy, though I guess the way I act comes off as shyness. What I experience is different from what I imagine the average shy person experiences. It's more than social awkwardness, not knowing what to say, how to say it, or how to dance. What I and, I believe, others with ADHD often experience is intense fear and extreme anxiety.

Until very recently, I've been uncomfortable around kids my own age. Throughout nursery school, elementary school, middle school, and even the first couple years of high school, I often felt that I was not welcomed into a circle of friends because I felt I was not "normal." I felt that the behaviors that come with ADHD—particularly not waiting my turn, not being able to label or express my feelings, not following classroom procedures, blurting out answers or questions—would cause me to be excluded. I became pessimistic about friendships. I knew that even if kids accepted me at first, it was only a matter of time before they would turn away from me, the friendships would end, and I would be rejected from the group.

So, in response, I developed a protective mechanism. I would exclude myself—before anyone could exclude me. I avoided groups at lunch, dances at the middle school, going to the movies. I figured that if I never joined a group, I could save myself the anguish of being eventually—and always— rejected from that group. Predicting that I wouldn't make friends became a self-fulfilling prophesy. If you believe that something is true, you act a certain way to make it come true in the end—even if it wasn't true in the beginning.

You may be wondering why I assumed I would get rejected. I assumed it because I had been excluded so many times in the past. I was always the last one to be chosen, whether it was to be part of a Civil War research group in history, someone's partner to dissect a worm in a science lab, or a team member in PE. I would stand against the wall and watch how the kids doing the selection would avoid looking at me until they absolutely had to. I learned to go quickly to the water fountain so I would not suffer the embarrassment of being the last one in the class to be picked. So it was a learned habit. To prevent the agony of exclusion by others, I learned to exclude myself from the situation first.

How did I change? As I mentioned before, just because you have ADHD doesn't mean you have to go friendless. Change happened gradually, as I grew in maturity. I realized that a lot of my problems with making friends came from people reacting to my ADHD symptoms, which have an impact on basic social skills. Once I realized that, I began to do something about it, using some of the techniques I talked about in chapter 6: liking yourself, learning to pay attention, thinking before talking, slowing your impulsivity, and the ideas I mention here, especially making yourself get out there in the social scene.

⮕ solutions

If you suffer from social anxiety, the best way to tackle this problem is to confront it directly. You need to put yourself in social situations. Let other kids see that you are friendly, that you do want to join in, and that you do have talents to contribute to the school.

① **Find an excuse to say hi.** If you are a loner, you will be excluded. Don't be a quiet person in the background, because you may seem to be standoffish, instead of what you really are, which is shy.

It may seem like a really simple thing, but saying hello to classmates in the hallways can actually have a major, positive effect on kids. They will be aware that you exist and that you are friendly and worth talking to. Because I felt shy and awkward, I used to walk down the school hallways with my head down, ignoring people. But as I started to greet people, I found that it made it easier to have a conversation with them.

Next, find a reason to talk with someone. One good subject to talk about is homework, because everyone always has a lot to say about it. It is a guaranteed conversation starter. So, go ahead and discuss last night's homework: the fact that there was too much, that it was unfair, or that it didn't make sense.

This breaks the ice, and once you're talking, you'll feel more comfortable and continue talking about other things. You can ask where your classmate lives, if he or she has a pet, and brothers or sisters.

Siblings are another hot topic! Everyone likes to complain about brothers or sisters and how they get you into trouble. You can also talk to your classmates about movies, current events, famous people or just people in school, and so on. Read up on popular culture—for example, read *People* magazine and the sports pages—so that you can start a conversation. The list of topics is endless. Also, have IM and Facebook accounts on your computer and text messaging on your cell phone, so you can keep in touch with your friends outside of school hours and during vacations. As you find out more about your classmates, you'll be able to find common experiences to share.

② **Force yourself to join the group at the lunch table.** After you find a friend from class in the lunchroom, join that person and start talking about the class you have together. Take a baby step toward joining a group and build from there. Start talking with someone who is not threatening, someone who you know is friendly and will respond well to you. This is the first step. Next, you can approach and join others. If kids see that you are sociable at the lunch table, they will be willing to become your friend. When I started eating lunch with friends in high school, I met more and more people and then slowly befriended all of them. If you do not join groups, you'll be isolated. Kids will view you as a loner and avoid you even more. It is a self-perpetuating cycle.

③ **Do well in something.** People admire talent, whether it's in a school subject, the arts, a sport, or an extracurricular activity. When my classmates found out that I was good in chemistry, they looked up to me and respected me more than they had before. I even helped some of my friends with their work, and their respect for me grew.

I also joined the swim team. Kids in sports are considered strong, and other kids respect those who can win the swimming relay race or play a football game in ninety-degree heat. Furthermore, being on a sports team opens up more opportunities for friendships. At first, I didn't want to be on a sports team, because I feared that I would not get along with my teammates and that they would reject me for having ADHD. However, when I joined the swim team, I unexpectedly found that I had a ready-made network of new friends who couldn't care less if I had ADHD. They just cared about my 200-meter freestyle.

④ **Go to social events.** Don't make the same mistake I made. Become involved in your school culture and activities outside the classroom. This will give you a chance to learn more about your classmates. Go to dances, parties, movies, sporting events, and dinners. Being involved shows that you are sociable. It shows you are willing to be part of the community. A good thing to do is to go with a friend for moral support. When I began regularly attending dances and parties in high school, I met many people and became better friends with people I already knew.

Again, you will have to fight the urge to stay by yourself, to be quiet, to not volunteer. You need to face the fear of social contact if you're going to defeat it. Running away from anxiety will only make you more anxious the next time. Each time you force yourself to join in, it will become easier to join in the next time.

You will have to ignore the nerves and then and push yourself out there. And once you do, you will be rewarded. Make yourself join that first dance!

— 9 —

being misunderstood

calling in the experts preschool

I wake up on the white, foldout mattress in my parents' room. Although I have a room of my own, there are two problems with it. First, it's upstairs from their room and therefore too far from my parents, and, second, my curtains do not completely close. I worry that, without my mother's watchful gaze and protection, a Tyrannosaurus rex can easily peer into my window and eat me as a meal. I am four years old.

After skipping the required chore of hanging up my clothes and brushing my teeth before going to school, I go to breakfast. The water is running. Gloria is rinsing a bathing suit in the sink.

"Hi, Goria." I attempt to pronounce her name correctly, with the "l," but this accomplishment will have to wait another year.

"Ey, ey, you want some egg?" Gloria asks in her Trinidadian accent.

"Yes, please."

I sit down at the table in the kitchen and see an IBM press release that my mother's communications staff has written. I try to decipher the computer announcement. I see a multitude of business and high-tech words over ten letters long: reliability, availability, scalability. My feet dangle from the chair.

After the stove fan has thundered with ferocity for three minutes, Gloria puts my plate on top of a dinosaur mat with the T. rex.

Suddenly, I hear the click of my mother's high-heeled shoes coming down the hall.

"Okay, honey," my mother says, "Daddy's going to take you to school today. I have to go to work early."

"But, I don't want you to go," I say. I feel bad every time my mother leaves for work ahead of me.

"Well, Mommy has to go to work, honey bun. I have a big announcement today. I'm sorry." She adjusts her black suit. "But I promise we'll read one of the Thomas the Tank Engine books tonight when I get home."

"Okay, see you later, Gloria," she says.

"Bye, Nah-dine."

As I push my fork through the scrambled eggs to make egg shards, I hear loud footsteps. My father, when approaching me from the hallway, intentionally stomps his foot down, mimicking a T. rex. My father roars. It's a game that he will continue to play with me until I turn ten. However, at four years of age, the sound of a dinosaur does not seem out of place.

"Hi, Moosh!" My father greets me affectionately. This nickname is also our dog's nickname. He holds his hands in the air to imitate dinosaur claws, despite the fact that the T. rex's claws were very small compared to its body.

"You know what? It's time for S-C-H-O-O-L," he deliberately spells out the word for me slowly.

"Noooo...," I reply in disappointment.

"Hi, Stan," Gloria chuckles as she greets my father.

"Hi, Gloria, G-L-O-R-I-A," he says.

"Okay, Blake, we have to leave in seven minutes, at seven forty-seven," he says.

With his right hand, he now imitates the banking of a 747 plane, because a Boeing 747 is our favorite plane. He also does this when the clock shows 727, 737, 757, and 767. The Boeing 717 does not have the same lyrical rhythm as the other models, and so it is excluded.

Ten minutes later, we are in the white Jeep, and being mid-October, the snow and ice have not yet arrived, but the air has become frigid. As he straps me into the blue child seat in the back, he announces, "Okay, we're clear for takeoff!"

He turns on the engine and switches the gear into drive.

"Here we go. Rrrrrr…" He imitates the sounds created by an accelerating jet engine.

As we exit the driveway and turn onto our street, he says, "Okay, we're now cruising at thirty-eight thousand feet."

We pass by our quiet and reserved neighbors' homes. Since the houses sit on two-acre lots in Weston, Connecticut, we don't see our neighbors very often. When we do see them outside, they occasionally nod, but then they look away, not wanting to talk, preferring their privacy. Because the houses are far apart, nestled in the woods, a car is needed to carry trick-or-treaters from door to door. Otherwise, it would take all evening to cover just five homes.

More cars appear on the road as we approach the coastal town of Westport, and I become sad, thinking about how I dislike my school. I have told my parents several times that I dislike the Weston-Westport Cooperative Nursery School, my first preschool, but they just figure that I, like most kids my age, dislike leaving my home in the morning.

I have told my parents several times that I dislike my preschool, but they just figure that I, like most kids my age, dislike leaving my home in the morning.

As part of the boring daily drive, we cross a wooden hundred-year-old bridge over the Saugatuck River in the middle of town. It's adjacent to the preschool.

"Okay, Blake, we're almost there," my father says.

"Ohhh…" I exhale a sigh of annoyance.

As we approach the building, I watch the other parents walk their children into the beige building that is attached to a modern church. My father puts the Jeep in park and opens the door. The beeping, which signifies that a door is open, is incessant. He unbuckles me from the toddler seat, picks me up, and places my feet on the pavement.

"Let's go, come on," he says. He leaves the car door open.

As we enter the school's doors, the noise of children intensifies sharply. There are screeches, laughter, and the banging of plastic toy cars. I hold my hands over my ears as my father escorts me to my classroom.

"Bye, Moosh!" he says.

"Bye, Daddy," I reply.

Red, blue, and orange colors and bright fluorescent lights glitter in the room. Giant construction paper flowers are stuck to the wall, their petals curling outward. Checkerboard patterns. Halloween pumpkins. A shiny linoleum floor and the combined smell of milk and disinfectant.

My peers are gathered among the groups of small chairs and small tables, for arts and crafts is always first on the morning agenda. It is 8:05 A.M., and Miss Mary, as we call her because of her unpronounceable Russian last name, brings out the paper and paints.

The children wait expectantly at their tables like horses at the starting gate, waiting to bolt. As soon as the paints are placed on the table, the grabbing begins. Since we use our hands to paint, there is a loud, boisterous paint fight on a daily basis; all of our hands can't fit into a given paint jar at the same time.

George, a classmate seated next to me, shouts at another classmate, "I was here first!" He is referring to the blue paint jar.

"No, you weren't. My hand touched it first!" screeches another boy.

They attempt to each pull the paint jar toward themselves, but only succeed in keeping the jar trembling in midair between them. The blue paint splatters on the desk and floor.

"Come on, I wanna get the blue!" a third classmate cries out, annoyed that the fight between the two boys is delaying her painting. She joins in the argument.

Now, the three of them yell, shout, and tug at each other, and more paint spills on the floor. It bothers me a lot. You may think that I would have been used to this noise and that it wouldn't bother me. But this is not the case. The loud, sharp noises hurt my ears, unlike any other child's in the classroom. The other children either ignore the noises or don't hear the shrieks. I cannot simply ignore the noises; they are like needles piercing my eardrums, and they keep me from concentrating or thinking clearly. Miss Mary tries to calm the children, but as she is well aware, we are only four years old, and the yelling and screaming is simply going to continue.

The bright colors zigzag in front of my eyes. Everything is shiny and moving in a blur of patterns.

I can't take it anymore, and I try to think of what to do. Since the class (and the noise) is concentrated in three sections of the room, where the boys are playing with dinosaurs, the girls with Barbie dolls, and still others with pots and pans, I decide to remove myself from the confusion. I go to build blocks in the opposite corner of the classroom, where it is quiet and where I can be alone. I decide to build a city of buildings, bridges, and tunnels with wooden building blocks. I am able to avoid the ear-piercing noise. I literally concentrate so hard on my designs that I am able to shut out all the noise around me. I can't even hear the teacher calling me.

> The loud, sharp noises hurt my ears, unlike any other child's in the classroom. They are like needles piercing my eardrums, and they keep me from concentrating or thinking clearly.

"Hey, Blake, Blake!" Miss Mary has called me three times, but I haven't heard her. She comes over to tap me on the shoulder. "How about playing dinosaurs with us over there?" she asks, pointing to a group of children seated on the floor around the couch.

"No, I don't want too," I answer and turn back to my building.

"Oh, it's fun," Miss Mary says. "Won't you come?"

"No, I don't like it," I say abruptly and start to turn away again.

I notice that Miss Mary frowns before going back to her group.

Later in the day, our nursery school principal enters the room. Miss Mary goes over to her and points me out. The principal looks at me building my structures alone in the corner of the room while all the other kids are gathered in groups. I am the only one playing alone. My teacher and the principal watch me intently and look concerned. They turn to whisper to each other, and the principal nods and turns to leave the classroom.

From that day on, I continue to isolate myself with my wooden blocks, working on city designs in the corner of the classroom.

My classmate Tucker comes over to me in the corner.

"What are you doing, Blake?" he asks, smiling, but his smile has an edge of malice to it.

I begin to answer, but then his foot goes backward and swings forward.

Woosh! With one kick, my city is shattered.

I am angry and pick up a block and throw it at him, hitting him on the forehead. He screams.

"Blake hit me!" Tucker cries as he holds his head and looks over toward the teacher.

I stand there speechless and red faced, with a block in my hand. I drop the block.

"Blake, what did you do?" Miss Mary scolds.

She removes both of us from the classroom so that we can explain what happened.

My mother takes me to school the next morning and goes in to see the principal. She comes out after an hour and gives me a kiss good-bye, but I notice that her eyes are red and a little wet.

Not long after, on a winter day in January, two new adults visit the classroom.

"Okay, class, this is Miss Martins and Miss Arlene," Miss Mary introduces them.

"They're going to be with us for a couple days," Miss Mary says, but she doesn't tell us why.

"Can we all say, 'Hi, Miss Martins'?"

"Hi, Miss Martins," the class repeats. Miss Martins waves her hand.

"And hello to Miss Arlene."

"Hello, Miss Arlene," the class sings.

Like Miss Mary, Miss Arlene also has an unpronounceable Russian last name, and so everyone calls her by her first name.

I notice that Miss Arlene and Miss Martins do not teach or help Miss Mary with the other children, as other visiting adults do. Instead, they seem to stay near where I am, near my corner with the wooden blocks. They sit in their adult chairs and ask me about my city designs. They watch me, take notes, whisper between each other, and nod. I wonder why they don't ask the other children about their projects.

Soon after the visit from Miss Martins and Miss Arlene, I find out why they were there. It concerned me and the fact that I am to be transferred out of the cooperative nursery school and into the public preschool into Miss Arlene's class. This is all right with me.

Miss Arlene's class consists of only six children and three instructors. The room is spacious and orderly. It is quiet and peaceful. No screaming is allowed. There is only quiet discussion at the round tables, as Miss Arlene patiently explains numbers, cloud formations, and the different species of birds to us. All the books are lined up by size on their shelves. Every student has a cubicle with his or her name on it, with hooks for our jackets. There are couches and pillows in the reading corner. Toys are lined up under the window. I can finally relax, learn, and do projects. I befriend the children. One boy is in a wheelchair, another has crutches, and a third has problems talking.

At the end of the year, I am sorry to leave Miss Arlene's class for kindergarten.

cause & effect

Years later, my mother told me what had happened at the Weston-Westport Cooperative Nursery School. My teacher Miss Mary and the principal had requested that the Weston school district administrators come and observe me because they suspected I had severe developmental problems. After several days of observation, the school administrators suspected that I might have autism, a disorder in which kids seem withdrawn and may not make eye contact with people, may not talk or play the way other children do, or may repeat certain motions and behaviors (American Academy of Family Physicians 2007). They assigned me to a special needs class for mentally and physically challenged children. One of my classmates in the new class could not communicate, another had no control of his body functions, and a third was paralyzed. At the time, I didn't realize the full extent of their limitations. I just thought of them as other kids.

The irony of this story is that the school administrators thought that there was something seriously wrong with me when, in fact, a big part of the problem was the environment into which I had been placed initially. It's true, I have ADHD, but a classroom with yelling, shouting, bright fluorescent lights, and confusion isn't for everyone—and a classroom like that was an especially big problem for someone with my condition. As my mother said, even she got a bad headache when she helped out in the nursery school classroom.

School administrators have to be more aware of ADHD and some of the basic requirements of kids with ADHD. There are an estimated four million of us in the United States with ADHD, and a few simple changes can help us a lot. This condition is frequently misunderstood and misdiagnosed. In

> School administrators have to be more aware of ADHD. There are an estimated four million of us in the United States with ADHD, and a few simple changes can help us a lot.

fact, many people still doubt it is a real thing, believing ADHD is not a legitimate condition but, instead, an excuse for a badly behaved child or for poor parenting. People who believe that are wrong. You may be hyperactive and impulsive if you are bored or if there is a lot of confusion in the classroom. You may have problems in school if you can't concentrate or focus. You may act out as a result of some of these problems, and then this acting out may create secondary problems with your classmates. You may isolate yourself if you can't cope, or if you can't make friends, and this will turn you into a loner.

One very real characteristic of ADHD is what is called tactile sensitivity. That means you are extremely sensitive to bright lights, loud sounds, tastes and textures, touch and smell (National Resource Center on ADHD 2007). This is why I hated the fluorescent lights and the bright colors and noise of the preschool. This is why I'm sensitive about hugs.

After moving to Miss Arlene's class, I began to participate in all the activities with the other children. But I still continued to build the wooden structures, not because I needed to avoid intolerable noise levels but because I had developed an interest in constructing things—a hobby which exists to this day. I would stack the wooden arches and cubes on top of one another to make a building that would stay standing, and the idea of creating larger and stronger block structures motivated me to continue to build.

But after Miss Arlene's class, in kindergarten, I began to isolate myself again from my classmates. Up until about fourth grade, I spent every recess after lunch in the library writing reports. I would read a book and then handwrite a report on the subject. I wrote a total of three reports. The first, named "The Planets," was 101 pages long (I wrote in big letters toward the end so I could reach 101 pages), the second, named "Trains, Airplanes, and Bridges," was 57 pages long, and the third, named "The Sea," was 201 pages. I would go to the library with a friend of mine, named Laura, who would voluntarily read books and take notes with me. I later discovered that Laura, like myself, also had ADHD. I think we were both trying to find a quiet and accepting place, a place where we could be safe. As a result, our classmates, who played on the playground, viewed us as loners and excluded us.

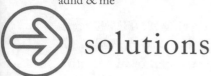

solutions

When I was very young, ADHD was still a mostly unknown condition and it frequently went undiagnosed. There were no television or magazine ads for medications for it. There were no magazines devoted to it or summer camps just for kids with ADHD. A lot of people know about it now, but there is still a lot of doubt about the subject. In a major *New York Times* article about childhood psychiatric conditions, Benedict Carey wrote that determining what is wrong is "more of an art than a science. Psychiatrists have no blood tests or brain scans to diagnose mental disorders. They have to make judgments based on interviews and checklists of symptoms" (Carey 2006). Knowing this, you will have to realize that you and your parents are your best advocates. If you read my stories and see parts of yourself in them, it is up to you and your family to get the assistance you will need. To avoid being misunderstood, check out the following solutions.

(1) **Tell your school about your ADHD.** School administrators, counselors, and teachers are not doctors. Do not expect them to know that you have ADHD unless you tell them. Obviously, your parents will need to meet with them to discuss it. The school counselor will probably need to talk to your doctor. Make sure your teachers are well aware of your condition, because they will then understand what to do to help you. Just like you wouldn't expect someone with a broken right arm to write, they shouldn't expect you to do things you can't do. Don't let them guess. Once I was diagnosed with ADHD, my mother would meet with teachers at the beginning of each school year so that they fully understood my ADHD and what accommodations would make it easier for me to learn and cooperate in the classroom.

(2) **Know your rights.** ADHD is a recognized condition, and you can have a special plan in place, just for you, at school. They call it an individualized education plan, or IEP. The plan

lists your skills and talents and the things you need to improve. It also lists what your teachers can do to help you improve, including the following: have you sit in the front row, so you can pay better attention; make sure you hear the assignments; ask you to repeat the assignment so that they know you heard the request; help you get organized by ensuring you have the right books and notes for homework and exams; allow you to stand in the back of the room if you are feeling restless in class; go for a drink of water if you need a break; find projects that interest you and will engage your creativity; and give you a quiet place and extra time for tests. Having an IEP can make all the difference in how successful you are in school (National Resource Center on ADHD 2007).

③ **Be in small, quiet classrooms.** I cannot emphasize this enough. I did well in my subjects when I learned and studied in small, quiet, and interactive classrooms. Big schools with many students in a class have worked against me. As my doctor, Jean Paul Marachi, told my mother, "Instead of increasing Blake's medicine so he can function in a large classroom, put him into a small classroom that is better suited for him, where he won't have all the distraction and noise." My mother followed his advice, and it worked. I suggest that you ask your parents to enroll you in a school that can provide you with a small learning environment. As part of this, as you get older, you can also ask to take exams in small, quiet rooms, as opposed to large classrooms or gymnasiums with many kids. Less distraction means you'll be better able to concentrate.

④ **Don't be shy: ask for changes in the classroom.** Specify to the teachers what aspects of the classroom you like and what you do not like. If you need a larger desk, ask for a larger desk. If you need more paper while taking an exam, ask for more paper. If you need help with note-taking, ask. If you don't ask, it won't happen. As long as your requests aren't extreme and your changes do not hinder another classmate's ability to learn, your teacher can meet your requests. If your teacher says no, ask your parents for assistance.

(5) **Ask for the kind of teacher who is best for you.** I have found that my best teachers were those who were strict and firm but also nurturing, helpful, organized, and in possession of a good sense of humor. They kept me focused on a given assignment but were flexible and understood my condition. Netta Maclean, my high school math teacher, would remind me gently if she saw I was not paying attention to the algebra equations. Then she would ask me to do a problem right away, or she would say she was going to check my class work immediately after the lecture. Robert Stewart, my high school IB biology teacher, nurtured my interest in cell biology. He patiently allowed me to investigate the effect of sound (instead of light) on wasp larvae, and he didn't flinch when I put my iPod earbuds on the larvae to see their reactions. As Mr. Stewart said, "Blake, the burden of the proof is on you. You need to find the research that supports your theory. If you can do that, I'll go along with you." Tony Ignatius, my classical piano teacher, taught me to appreciate and play the works of Mozart, Beethoven, and Chopin. We debated interpretations of Chopin's nocturnes and the "Black Key" Étude. He listened to what I had to say and he gave me artistic freedom where he could, but he was also steadfastly demanding when I needed to follow the protocol of the music. These teachers worked with me, not against me, patiently guiding me throughout. They were able to excite my curiosity in many subjects and give me the freedom to do projects in unique ways.

(6) **A website just for you: www.help4adhd.org.** The CHADD National Resource Center on ADHD is a national, nonprofit organization providing lots of information and support for us. Its website has fact sheets, news, questions

and answers, and advice about treatment, educational issues, and living with ADHD. The organization also has chapters throughout the country.

You and your parents need to ask for things that can help you. Remember, though, you are your own best expert.

— 10 —

being blamed

the wicked witch of Hurlbutt 1st grade

"When something happens in the past, you take away the ending of the word and add an 'ed,'" Mrs. Perril explains as she holds a piece of chalk in her hand. I'm in first grade at Hurlbutt Elementary School in Connecticut, and Mrs. Perril is my teacher.

"If the word already has an 'e' in the ending, such as the word, 'like,'" she adds, as she writes LIKE on the chalkboard, "you take away the 'e' and add 'ed.' You don't just add a 'd.'"

I sit in my chair, bored and restless, anxiously waiting for the recess bell to ring. I reach into my wooden desk, find a blue pen, and throw it at the wall. The pen explodes as it hits the wall, splashing ink on some of Mrs. Perril's papers. My classmates gasp and then laugh. Mrs. Perril whirls around from the chalkboard, doesn't even look at the wall, and stares directly at me. I am the usual suspect.

"Blake, what did you just do?" she asks sharply.

I don't answer.

Mrs. Perril looks first at the splash of ink on the wall and then at her desk.

"You threw the pen! Do you want to go to the principal's office?" she asks, pointing with her white chalk in the direction of Dr. T's office. I shake my head no.

"No recess for a week because of what you just did." She looks at her papers splattered with blue ink and then quickly writes herself a note about my punishment so that she won't forget.

Mrs. Perril is a harsh first-grade teacher who believes that strict, old-fashioned discipline and force is the best way to handle children. She is slender with brunette hair. Since it is April, she knows her first-grade students well, and she is convinced that I am the one headed for delinquency and who should be disciplined the harshest. It doesn't matter that my mother has met with Mrs. Perril to discuss my ADHD and the methods used to control it. She seems to dismiss the condition as an excuse for my bad behavior. She is not going to change. She is determined that I will change. She will *make* me behave.

The recess bell rings.

"Okay, you may leave for recess; fifteen minutes" Mrs. Perril states as if disappointed that her students are allowed a break.

I still want to go out for recess and am willing to be sneaky to get it. Since I am near the door of the classroom leading directly to the playing field, all of my classmates have to walk past me. As the crowd approaches, I get up and start walking

> It doesn't matter that my mother has met with Mrs. Perril to discuss my ADHD and the methods used to control it. She seems to dismiss the condition as an excuse for my bad behavior.

toward the door, hoping that Mrs. Perril will not notice me among a crowd of twenty first-graders. But she can't be fooled. She watches me like a hawk.

"Blake, come back here!" she yells, as I am about to go out the door.

"I told you, no recess. You are being punished. Don't try to avoid it," she says in a punitive tone. "Now, because you tried to sneak out, your punishment is going to be increased. In addition to losing recess for the remainder of this week, you will not have recess on Monday and Tuesday of next week." She makes a note about my new punishment on her calendar.

I look down at my desk in disappointment and fiddle with a pencil and ruler inside my desk. I will not have a break for more than a week because I have thrown a pen. This is torture. I want so much to go outside and run around. It is finally springtime in Connecticut. I look out the window and watch the other kids climb on the bright blue jungle gym, slide down slides, and play kick ball.

After fifteen minutes or so, my classmates reenter the classroom, glowing with the warmth of exercise from the sunny spring day outside. I sit at my desk with my head down.

After a short lunch break and another grammar lesson, that magic time, three fifteen, has finally arrived. I can escape from Mrs. Perril. I hate school.

"All class stand, and then you may leave," Mrs. Perril announces as the bell rings. In order to avoid an awkward, one-on-one encounter with her, I am the first to leave.

I walk toward the bus circle, where six long yellow buses idle with their engines running. Each bus has a planned route, meandering among the dense pine trees. I get on bus number 25, which will travel to my section of Weston.

The bus driver, whose name is Ed, is older, corpulent, and a somewhat monklike character. Every day, he has to endure the screeching of the children in the bus. The old brown bus seats have been ripped over time, and to mend them, Ed has applied duct tape of approximately the same color. The older kids, notably the third-graders, have the unofficial privilege of sitting in the back of the bus, while the youngest, which include me and the other first-graders, sit in the front, closer to Ed. My house is only a fifteen-minute drive by car from school, but the bus ride, which includes dozens of stops, takes an hour. Start. Stop. Start. Stop. It is a miserable end to a miserable day. I prefer to sit alone, trying to block out the noise, and look out the window at the spring buds.

Finally, at about four fifteen, we arrive at my house.

"Twenty-six Walker Lane," Ed announces in a hoarse voice.

I eagerly get out of my seat and walk toward the door of the empty bus.

"Good-bye. Thank you," I say to Ed.

"See you tomorrow," he says as he smiles and tips his hat.

I walk up the driveway to my house. The bus turns around, with its back-up warning beeping, in the cul-de-sac behind me. As I approach the kitchen door, I see Gloria's face in the window as she unlocks it.

"'Allo, sweetie!" Gloria greets me. "How was school today?" she asks, her dark brown eyes sparkling as she gives me a big hug.

I give the typical, expected answer: "Good."

"Okay, then, you go watch TV, and I'm gunna cook you a nice dinna," she says as she guides me toward the TV and picks up a broom.

I turn on the Weather Channel, my favorite television station, and watch the weather across the country for the next several hours.

My father arrives home first, at about six thirty, and then my mother an hour later. Shortly after, they call me to their room. I enter the bedroom, which is somewhat dark, and see both of them standing together, silhouetted in their suits, with their arms crossed.

"I got a call from your teacher today," my mother says. "Apparently, you threw many pens in the classroom and splattered ink all over the room."

"Oh god!" I think to myself, "Mrs. Perril did *not* actually call my house because I threw a pen."

"And we're very disappointed in you," my father adds.

But wait a minute, I think to myself. I realize that the story my mother just told me is not what actually happened.

"Okay, first of all, I only threw one pen, and that's because her class is so boring," I say to my parents, as they stare at me. "And that probably wasn't right, but I didn't throw *many* pens."

"Well, that's not what Mrs. Perril said," my mother says. "Do you want to hear the message?"

"Okay," I say.

She turns on the answering machine, and I hear Mrs. Perril exaggerating the pen-throwing incident to make it seem a lot more serious than it was. It is as if she wanted to turn my parents against me.

"That's a lie!" I yell.

Although my parents trust me and know I don't lie, I realize that being only six years old, I don't have the credibility of an adult. In effect, Mrs. Perril has the power to say what she wants, to embellish the truth, and my parents will believe her just because she is a teacher and an adult. It's so unfair.

"Well, you're going to time-out for one hour in your room," my mother tells me.

My father grasps me firmly by the arm and then escorts me out the door and into my room as if I were a juvenile delinquent. I am being punished a second time that day for the one incident. On top of that, I am being punished for throwing *many* pens—not just one—and I didn't even hit anyone! I realize I was wrong to throw the pen to begin with and to create a stir in the classroom, but I don't feel I should be punished over and over. I sit in my room and think about how Mrs. Perril is using this pen-throwing incident as a means of demonstrating her power and its reach into my home. She is showing who is boss.

Ed picks me up at seven forty-five the next morning. Since I am one of the last students to be dropped off in the afternoon, I am also among the last to be picked up in the morning. The bus is already crowded, and the kids are screaming and arguing. I manage to find a seat by myself. As Ed drives to school, I look out the window and think about my dislike for Mrs. Perril. I try to ignore the talking and screaming. I hate going to her class. Who knows what confrontation will happen today?

By 8:10 A.M., I enter Mrs. Perril's classroom. When the entire class has arrived, she has us all stand up and, as a daily routine, look at the flag to recite the Pledge of Allegiance.

"I pledge allegiance to the flag, of the United States of America..."

For the remainder of the morning, Mrs. Perril slowly continues her lessons about the past tense. She includes irregular past-tense verbs, such as "think," "see," and "drive," which become "thought," "saw," and "drove." As the midmorning break approaches, the rest of my classmates start fidgeting.

"Okay, everyone stand," Mrs. Perril orders, "and all, except for Blake, may go to recess."

My classmates look at me, point, and giggle. One boy makes a face at me. They line up, as if it were a military drill, and exit the door. After they have left the room, Mrs. Perril and I are alone together. After about a minute, she speaks.

"Blake, get up. You're coming with me," she orders.

She stands up, tucks her brunette hair behind her ear, and leads me out of the classroom into the hallway.

"Follow me," she says in a firm tone. Her floor-length, flowered dress sways behind her.

She takes me to the one-person bathroom and opens the door. Inside the bathroom, there is urine all over the toilet seat, as well as the tiled floor, the walls, and even the handicapped bar. "What a mess!" I think to myself.

"Did you do this?" she asks, but seems sure of the answer before getting my reply.

"No," I respond.

"Oh, yes, you did," she says. "And you're going to clean it up." A sly smile appears on her face.

"What? But I didn't do it," I cry out.

"Yes, you did!" She says it with glee. She must be thinking, "I've got him now. He's going to learn a lesson that he'll never forget."

She leaves the bathroom for a minute or so and returns with paper towels and a mop from the janitor's office.

Unlike the pen throwing, when I was guilty of creating an incident, the bathroom mess was *not* my doing. I am enraged because it's clear that she blames me any time something goes wrong. She is using this incident to exercise one of her severe discipline tactics. Being only six years old, I do not think of going to the principal to tell my side of the story. More importantly, I don't know that it wouldn't be right to make a child clean urine off bathroom walls and fixtures, even if I were the culprit. But Mrs. Perril has absolute power at this point and is itching to use it. She wants to humiliate me.

"She's a witch," I think. "A wicked witch!"

I am trapped. There is nothing else that I can do except clean the bathroom. I begin mopping the floor, smelling the sharp odor of stale urine in the air. I feel sick to my stomach because of the odor and because of the humiliation. As Mrs. Perril watches from outside the bathroom with her arms crossed, she orders me to use the paper towels to clean the toilet seat and the walls. As I clean off the urine, some of it soaks through the paper towels and reaches the skin on my hands. I clean the toilet seat, noticing the company's name, American Standard, written along the side.

After ten minutes, I am finished cleaning the bathroom. I immediately wash my hands after Mrs. Perril tells me to throw the paper towels in the garbage. The Wicked Witch, as I now think of her, leads me back toward the classroom. I sit down at my desk as she opens the door for all my classmates, who rush back happily into the room. What angers me the most is not that I've had to clean up a bathroom mess that I did not create; it's that no one will believe that I was forced to do so.

I ride home on the bus with Ed again, feeling angry, sad, and, most of all, defeated. I am also afraid that Mrs. Perril will call the house again, making up another story about how I was to blame for the bathroom mess. I check the answering machine as soon as I get in the door. Luckily, there's no message.

I decide not to tell my parents or Gloria about the incident, because I don't want to risk being punished again so soon after last night's punishment. I decide not to bring up the situation and hope that Mrs. Perril will not call.

When my parents come home that evening and ask how school was, I reply, "Good." I won't tell my mother about the incident for four more years, long after I have entered fifth grade.

cause & effect

I do admit that I have done plenty of mischievous things, as you know from my earlier stories: I have broken windows, set the kitchen table on fire, and launched rockets into tennis matches. Mrs. Perril was aware that I had ADHD and that I had more than my share of mishaps. As a result, she was quick to blame me whenever any trouble occurred; she automatically assumed that I had caused the trouble, whether or not she had proof of my involvement.

Those of us with ADHD may have an undeserved reputation for being the cause of *all* trouble, and so we are often the scapegoats. But while I have been in trouble frequently, the cause is often accidental. I am not trying to be mean, as some skeptics have come to believe about hyperactive children. I am just restless, bored, annoyed, awkward, or impulsive. I don't think about my actions before I do them, and many unintended mishaps occur.

Mrs. Perril made me into a scapegoat. My friends, other teachers, and even my parents also tended to blame me whenever something went wrong. If chemicals were spilled or a flask broken in chemistry lab, the teacher would immediately look in my direction. If the wall was marked or if something went missing at home, my parents would call from wherever they were in the house and say, "Blake, what did you do?" One time, we

> Those of us with ADHD may have an undeserved reputation for being the cause of *all* trouble, and so we are often the scapegoats.

were in Bloomingdale's and the alarms sounded. My mother's automatic reaction was "Blake! Stop!" I was always to blame.

In middle school, I would get a drink of water at the fountain on a regular basis (and sometimes fill my water bottle to squirt people). One day, the handle broke on the water fountain. Everyone, classmates and teachers, blamed me, just because they had seen me at the water fountain so often. The bottom line is that most people assume those with ADHD are always the cause of the trouble—even if we are not.

→ solutions

Kids with ADHD tend to have a history of odd and impulsive behaviors (National Resource Center on ADHD 2007). When confronted about a problem, these kids don't know how to speak up for themselves or how to defend themselves against the charges. Everyone tends to believe they are to blame because of their ADHD behaviors. Often, ADHD kids will get angry, blow up, storm off, or say something inappropriate to an authority figure because they are being unjustly accused. When this happens, the accuser then believes these kids must be guilty, because why else would they get so upset and argue? So, if that's the problem, what do you do about it?

① **Be a lawyer and present your case.** Authority figures, like teachers or parents, may seem overwhelming. You may think that because they are older, they are always right and what they say is automatically true. This is not the case; they are human and can make mistakes. Do not believe that because you are young, you cannot defend yourself and disagree with the accuser. Provide reasons as to why what they accuse you of cannot possibly be true. For instance, when the teacher in chemistry blamed me for breaking a flask, I pointed out that my breaking it was impossible because I was on the opposite side of the room at the time.

I caution you, however, to state your case firmly but courteously. Don't be argumentative or rude. This will make the other person angry, and he or she will be even more convinced that you are to blame.

② **Be honest.** If you are open and honest and tell the truth often, your accuser will be more likely to believe what you say. When I got into predicaments with classmates at school, the administration would generally believe my side of the story, since they knew that I was honest. So, don't lie.

③ **Bring in the reinforcements.** Because you are young, teachers or parents will often overpower you. In this case, use your adult allies. If there is trouble with a teacher, for instance, use your parents as leverage to combat the problem. If you have a dispute with your parents, often grandparents or close family friends can make reliable allies. Find a trusted adult who can help present your point of view.

④ **Know that sometimes it's just not fair.** I wish I could say that problems always get resolved and that people are always fair in the end, but that isn't the case. There are going to be times when you are treated unfairly. The good news is that this happens to everyone, whether you have ADHD or not. Sometimes you'll just have to get through a hard patch and say to yourself, "This will pass."

Because you have ADHD, you may have more than your share of incidents, but remember that how you deal with them can make all the difference. Everyone has his or her own witches to contend with.

being rigid

running the mile 7th grade

"Three minutes!" my PE teacher, Mr. Martin, calls out.

I look down at my white sneakers as I run the eight-lap mile. I don't feel that my mouth is wide enough to breathe in as much air as my lungs crave. Furthermore, the harsh June sun takes its toll on me, and I begin to sweat profusely.

"Come on folks, let's go! Show me some good times; make me happy!" Mr. Martin yells.

I feel like complaining about this seemingly pointless part of the school curriculum to my friend running on my right side, but I can't catch my breath long enough to speak a word.

"Three thirty," I hear Mr. Martin, a slender man in his midfifties, call in the distance as I near the starting point.

"Three forty-five."

"Four," he yells as I pass the checkpoint. I've only completed three of eight laps, but despite the fact that the student record is 5 minutes 54 seconds for eight laps, I don't care about my mile time or my grade in the class. I feel that PE is unnecessary.

"I hate this!" I yell as I pass Mr. Martin.

"Just keep going, Blake," he yells back.

People begin to finish the exercise when I am only halfway done, and so it's embarrassing to be one of the last to complete the mile.

End the torture.

Five laps, seven minutes, and a sore throat later, I finally finish this grueling task. The mile is a cornerstone of my middle school's PE agenda, and I have utter aversion to the class and particularly the running. At the beginning of every school year, I've painted an anti-PE sign on my rolling backpack (like the one displayed at left). This is intended to show my dislike for the class and also to give me an excuse for not doing well in it. I refuse to accept exercise as an essential part of life, and so I do not perform well during PE.

After everyone has finished the mile, Mr. Martin leads the class down a short dirt trail to the gym, where he plans to put us through another grueling exercise. After I've drunk what seems to be enough water to fill a small pond several times over, he gathers us in a group and announces our next activity.

"Well, you've caught your breaths and you've drunk your water, so now we're gonna do pull-ups on the bars." He sounds like a military drill sergeant.

I breathe a sigh of annoyance as I check the clock, waiting for that magical sound of the bell. Pull-ups, although not as bad as running, are painful and, in fact, even more embarrassing. I wait in line as the pull-up test is done, one by one, in front of everyone.

"Okay Blake, your turn," Mr. Martin calls out.

"I hate this," I respond.

"Too bad; get on the bars."

I stand under the pull-up bar and look up at it with some fear and annoyance. I jump up at the bar and manage to grab it. My classmates watch.

"All right, pull up," Mr. Martin calls.

I begin to lift myself upward, inching my way up toward the bar, but halfway there, I get stuck. I try with all my might to contract my triceps and deltoid muscles, until my arms began to shake under the strain. But eventually, despite my efforts, the muscle burn gets the better of me, and I am forced to release my grip, falling to the ground. No one laughs, but I am embarrassed. I'm embarrassed because, as a guy, I can't lift my own weight. Being embarrassed only makes me want to avoid PE all the more. Mr. Martin jots down a note in his grading book.

The mile is a cornerstone of my middle school's PE agenda, and I have utter aversion to the class and particularly the running.

"Next," he calls, without a word of encouragement for me.

As I lie in bed waiting to fall asleep that night, I think about how I want to be strong. But I also know that becoming strong would require a lot of time and effort, and I'm not sure I'd get the results I want anyway.

On a Saturday soon after the school incident, my mother wants to take my sister and me to the gym.

"Blake and Madison, we're leaving for the gym at twelve thirty," Mimi announces as we eat breakfast.

"I told you, I don't want to go," I reply.

"Yeah, I know, seriously," Madison adds.

"It's a nice day out, and we're going to go exercise," my mother says. "You are not going to just stay in front of the computer all day."

"I don't want to go," I insist. I am not going to go and make a fool of myself in the gym.

"Well, if you don't come, no computer for a week," my mother says.

"Come on Mom, we don't want to go!" Madison says.

"You have twenty minutes to get ready," my mother announces as she heads to her room to get dressed.

Madison and I go downstairs to watch twenty more minutes of the Discovery Channel. Meanwhile, I've conceived of a plan to avoid going to the gym by making my mother run out of time.

My mother and stepfather are planning to have dinner that evening with our neighbors at seven thirty. I calculate that in order for them to be at the restaurant on time, my mother will have to start getting ready at five o'clock because of the time it takes her to dry her long hair. If I can delay our leaving for the gym long enough, my mother will not have time for the gym.

I plan to begin taking a shower at 12:28 P.M., two minutes before my mother will come downstairs to summon Madison and me to go to the gym. Suddenly, I hear Mimi's footsteps coming down the stairs. I hop off the couch and go into my bathroom and turn on the shower.

I hear a knocking on the bathroom door.

"Blake?" I hear Mimi call through the door.

"Blake? Are you in there?"

"What?" I yell, the water from the shower obstructing my voice. "I can't hear you."

"Get out right now, or I'll send Ben in to get you."

Reluctantly, I get out of the shower and get dressed as slowly as I can, trying to take up as much time as possible. By the time I arrive in the kitchen, it's 12:44 P.M.

"Come on, get in the car," Mimi says. Madison and I obey, but we intentionally take slow steps.

"I can't believe we are being kidnapped and taken to the gym," I say to my sister.

For what seems like the entire twenty-minute car ride, my mother chides me for being unable to be on time. Finally, the three of us arrive at the gym.

"So, Blake, I made an appointment with a trainer to show you how to work out and lift weights," Mimi explains as she pulls into a parking space.

"What? You've got to be kidding me. This is ridiculous!"

"It's for your own good," Mimi replies.

We enter the gym and are greeted by air-conditioning and the faint smell of sweat. A trainer named Mark comes over to help us. A muscular man in his twenties, Mark seems to view the gym in the same way that a material girl views a shopping mall. His attitude is friendly and casual, which makes me feel a little better.

"So, Blake, what we're going to do today is start with cardio on the elliptical and then do weightlifting in many forms," he says, as my mother leaves.

The low whirr of people on step machines fills the background.

"So, we're going to do twenty minutes on the elliptical machine first," he says, looking up from his clipboard.

I frown as I get on the elliptical machine. It reminds me of running the mile at school. Mark sets the resistance and says that he will check back every three minutes. Surprisingly, the elliptical has a built-in television, and as I watch a program about the Antarctic, my dislike for exercising begins to decrease.

"Well, how was it?" Mark asks as I step off the machine.

"Not as bad as I thought it would be," I say, wiping the sweat off my face with a white towel. He looks at his list again.

"Now, we're going to do bench-pressing," he announces.

"Oh, is that the thing with the bar?" I ask.

"Yes, it is; it's the bread and butter of weightlifting."

My father is an avid bench-presser, and I have watched him work out on numerous occasions. I, however, never envisioned myself lifting the bar. Mark and I approach a bench.

"So, what you do here is put the weights on each side of the bar equally, and then lie down and push the bar up and down. I'll help you with it the first time."

I lie down on the bench and then become slightly intimidated by the sight of a forty-five-pound metal bar suspended over my chest.

"I think we'll start with just the bar before we start putting on weights," Mark says.

"Okay, then."

Mark stands behind the bench and grips the bar with his hands as I reach to grab it from below. He lifts the bar out of the notch and into midair, suspended over my chest.

"So, this is an easy concept. You let the bar come down slowly until it touches your chest." He brings the bar down until it touches my chest. "And then lift it up almost until your arms lock, and then repeat the process."

He lifts the bar up and down twice so that I will understand the correct procedure. Dance music plays in the background.

"Now, Blake, it's your turn to try it without my help."

He put his hands on the bar for safety purposes, but assures me that I will be doing the lifting. I take in a deep breath, look at the bar with determination, and then put my hands on it. I suddenly feel powerful.

"Ready, and, lift!" he says.

I apply force to the bar, and as I lift it halfway, I feel a flood of exuberance. I suddenly realize at this point that my stubbornness about exercise has been perhaps unfounded. I feel that, if I included working out into my routine, I could build muscle and become strong. Strength is good. At that moment, working out actually seems enjoyable.

I lift the bar eight more times afterward, and then Mark has me do other weightlifting exercises, such as biceps curls with dumbbells and weight-assisted pull-ups.

I leave the gym tired but feeling like I have accomplished something. My mother notices I look happy, and her eyes narrow as if to say, "I told you so."

> I apply force to the bar, and as I lift it halfway, I feel a flood of exuberance. I suddenly realize at this point that my stubbornness about exercise has been perhaps unfounded.

That night when I go to bed, I think about how I will make this new routine part of my daily life.

cause &effect

Rigidity is often a part of ADHD. I have always resisted trying anything new, be it exercising, going to a new place, such as a new park, beach, or museum, trying new clothes, getting up at a different time, or eating Mexican or Japanese food. It could even apply to reorganizing my books or rearranging furniture in my room. As my mother says, "Ask Blake to do something new, and he will always say no." Generally speaking, I don't like changing my routine or the things around me. I fear the result will be negative, almost as if something bad will happen. Because I feel something bad will happen, I don't take the risk of making the change. But the interesting thing is that once I am forced to try something new, and if I discover I like it, I will wholeheartedly embrace it.

Counselor George Lynn says this tendency to be rigid comes from a "desire to feel safe." An ADHD person will assume a "fortress mentality... to try to control his sense of inner chaos by assuming a decisional style of either-or. It is not perceived as safe to relax. It is a natural human reaction to feeling threatened or out of control." (1996, 93)

I was reluctant to exercise for the longest time. I just didn't want to do it, and I found many reasons not to do it. I didn't want to run or use workout equipment, because I would perspire, because I couldn't breathe right, because I had dust allergies, because I would get thirsty, or because my muscles would "burn." I didn't want to be locked into a schedule. To me, it was a big waste of time, and I had many other things I'd rather be doing. The bottom line is that I just didn't want to change. Once I realized that working out actually made me feel better and helped me become bigger and stronger, I decided it wasn't so bad after all, and I started an exercise routine all my own.

Being rigid like this has applied to foods also. For the first eleven years of my life, I would eat only five different kinds of food: cereal, meats, chicken, pasta, and pizza. I would eat the same foods over and over, at breakfast, lunch, and dinner and for snacks. One day, during a lesson on Japan in fifth grade, we had a class luncheon featuring sushi. When I finally tried the sushi, I decided I really liked it and then wanted to eat crab sushi all the time. I broke a record at a Japanese restaurant for eating thirty-eight pieces of crab sushi in one sitting, and the sushi chef had everyone applaud. Another example is chicken quesadillas. Like Japanese food, I didn't want to try Mexican food until I was forced to, and then I couldn't get enough of it, sometimes eating four large quesadillas at one sitting.

Another time, I decided I liked oranges, and I would go to great lengths to ensure I had them. We ran out of oranges one afternoon and, since my mother wasn't at home, I walked three miles to a grocery store and back to buy thirty oranges, which I ate as soon as I got home. I guess what I learned was that many of these new things were not as bad as I had initially thought. And, in fact, they turned out to be rather good for me.

→ solutions

If being rigid is a problem for you, too, you might want to try out some new things and experiences. You may be surprised at how much you enjoy them. Here's how you can do it.

(1) **Be open to something new.** When you are presented with something new, think positively. Don't reject it immediately just because it is new. When I look back, I realize I was mistaken not to exercise or to try a certain food. You will have to override your initial reaction to trying new things. You have to stop the negative thoughts about why something won't be good just because it is new. Try to think of the good effects that your change in routine could make. For instance, at first I really disliked PE, because it seemed to be a waste of time and

to require energy that could be better used doing something else. I read articles, though, that talked about the health benefits of exercise, and I focused on the fact that I could become stronger and fit. Suddenly, PE became something that could help me improve myself.

(2) **Get information.** I'm not saying that you must like every new place, food, or change in your routine, but you shouldn't reject things without knowing *something* about them. You need to do some research and make an intelligent and informed decision. For example, at first I resisted eating sushi, because I thought it was an unusual food that would taste bad. However, when I started to eat it, I read newspaper articles that talked about how sushi is healthy. I felt silly because I had dismissed it without knowing anything about it. The same thing could be said about trying a new sport or going to a new place. Learn about it and then decide.

Be open to new ideas and new experiences, because that new thing, instead of being bad, may be very good for you. You may even surprise yourself as you run that mile on your own!

— 12 —

being disobedient

spiders 12th grade

On a Saturday afternoon in late October, my friend Will and I decide to go sailing.

Will is the most recent addition to my senior class of 2007. Although he has moved to the Bay Area from France, and to France from Saudi Arabia, English was his first language. He was raised in the American enclave in Dhahran and has a Lebanese father and mother.

At the Stanford University sailing school, a large group of college students are racing FJs in the bay. When we arrive at the Stanford boathouse, the tall, athletic sailing director approaches us. "Hi, I'm Jay," he says. He's friendly but businesslike. "Alright, you know how to rig the boat? You know how to sail?"

"Yes," I answer. "I attended the sailing camp here for three summers."

"You know that you can sail only up to the point with the power lines, but not into the bay, right?" He gestures out toward the bay and then looks back at me. "And you know that you need to be in by four o'clock?"

I nod to show that I am familiar with the rules. Then he releases the boat to us.

"Alright, let's pull this boat out," I say to Will, making sure I have traction on the wet concrete floor of the boathouse. He reaches for the other handle of the trailer, and after we both give it a tug, the trailer moves forward with the boat.

"So, you've sailed here a lot?" Will asks. He isn't questioning my ability to sail but rather is asking out of curiosity. I am happy that I have his trust.

"For sure, many times," I answer.

He smiles. "Blake, this is gonna be so tight."

The day is sunny; the temperature is perhaps in the low sixties with light wind. I hope that more wind will come up as we rig the boat. We tie lines, raise sails, and close the drainage holes.

"We gotta give a name to this boat," Will says enthusiastically.

"How about," I pause to think, "how about Betty?" I raise my collar to protect my neck from sunburn.

"Alright. Betty it is," Will says as we launch the boat.

The Stanford dock is not located directly on the San Francisco Bay but on an inlet that leads to the bay more than a mile away. For three summers, I've learned how to sail here, and each summer, I've been determined to sail into the bay. Because it's windier out there, I think that bay sailing will be more exciting than sailing in a small, nondescript inlet. Sailing into the bay is prohibited, however, and every time I've tried to escape to the bay, a sailing instructor in a small white motorboat has pursued me and then scolded me for going beyond the limit. I've tried to escape so many times that I've learned how to set the sails perfectly to outrun the motorboats for a short distance. Today, the rule applies, but I am also well aware that the thirty or so college students racing a fleet of FJs are preoccupying the sailing director's attention. I may finally be able to escape.

When we are on a stable tack, the direction in which the boat sails, we take out our sandwiches and eat lunch. I keep one hand on the tiller to steer Betty. The wind is calm.

"Too bad there isn't a lot of wind," Will says, shading his eyes with his hand. He has forgotten his sunglasses.

"Yeah, I know. That's why we're going to the bay, where there's more wind."

"Wait. I thought the director said we aren't supposed to go into the bay," says Will.

"We're not," I say. "But we're going."

"Sweet," Will responds.

As we sail on, we pass a large docked tanker being loaded with bags of cement mix from a cement factory onshore. We sail close enough to the tanker to touch it. We realize its enormity, as it not only puts us in complete shadow but also towers several stories overhead, almost cutting off our wind.

The inlet, although relatively narrow, is dredged to accommodate tankers. I know we have to stay within the channel to keep away from the marshy bog known as Bair Island.

Every few minutes, I look over my shoulder, searching for a white motorboat heading in our direction at full speed, but all that is visible is a collection of small white FJs crisscrossing in the distance. We approach the power lines.

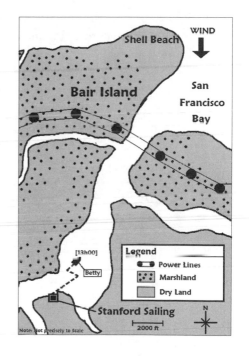

"Well, here's that famous point," Will says.

Overjoyed that I have made it this far without being caught, I say, "This is so exciting. We're actually evading the motorboats!" I look over my shoulder one last time to make sure.

As we enter the bay and pass Shell Beach on the left, the wind picks up, the waves become higher, and for the first time that day, I feel like I am really sailing. The scent of fresh, salty air fills our noses. I trim the mainsail, Will trims the jib, and we are off, into the bay. The bay seems like an enormous gift that's been kept hidden away by the sailing instructors.

About a mile out from shore, Will falls asleep at the jib in the warm afternoon sun. Suddenly, I see an object in the water perhaps fifty feet ahead of our boat. I sail closer.

"Will, look!" I shout. "It's a seal!"

The sight of the seal, which comes within five feet of Betty, adds to our sense of adventure. I glance over my shoulder and notice that the inlet leading to the sailing school is no longer visible on the horizon.

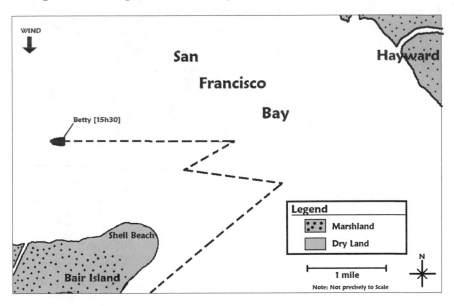

Although it's impossible to tell the exact time, since neither Will nor I have brought a watch, we figure it out by using the angle of the sun. Will holds up a stick, points it north, and then judges the length of the shadow to determine that it is approximately three thirty.

"Oh damn," I say. "We're supposed to be in by four." If we don't get back to the boathouse on time, I'll get caught having gone into the bay. I'm also aware that returning to port the way we came will take at least another two hours, and the wind is beginning to die down.

"How are we going to make it in time?" Will asks.

"I have an idea," I say. "We can take the inlet called the Corkscrew. It's a shortcut through Bair Island. It should get us there faster."

"Alright. Whatever you say, man," Will says as he sits back, relaxed.

Corkscrew, as the name suggests, is a winding inlet that can be, especially at low tide, a challenge to sail, because of the need to tack, or change the direction of the boat, continually. I've sailed the inlet before, and I know that it leads back to the Stanford sailing school. The problem, however, is that I've only sailed Corkscrew from the sailing school out to the bay, and not from the bay in. I can only guess what the entrance to Corkscrew will look like from the bay. I turn Betty toward shore, and when we're closer, I begin to cruise along the edge of Bair Island.

About fifteen minutes later, I find an inlet and enter it without hesitation. The inlet is narrow, long, and surrounded on both sides by tough, tan-colored marsh grass growing out from the submerged soil that is too thick to sail in yet too soggy to walk on. The marsh is a no-man's-land. In order to prevent becoming stuck, it's important that I keep the boat in the middle of the inlet.

Will and I quickly notice that the smell in the air has changed from a light, salty sea scent to a heavy, putrid odor. This is not a good sign, but I am optimistic that I have found Corkscrew, so we keep heading through the marshy island.

Bair Island is part of a salt marsh project in which Redwood City is reclaiming land from the bay and then building on the land. Since it is undergoing the gradual process of reclamation, the five-square-mile island is completely deserted.

"So, what types of food do you like?" I ask Will, as I try to take our minds off the predicament. Ironically, I'm talking about food even though we don't have any food or water on the boat.

"Well, French food is tight," he answers. His face shows a mix of uncertainty, excitement, and a slight amount of anxiety.

"In New York, the French restaurants are the best outside of France, but they're very expensive," I say.

"For sure."

As we continue the small talk, I notice what looks like a dead end ahead. I guess that it's actually one of the turns in the Corkscrew's winding course, and so I remain calm as we sail approximately a mile downwind into Bair Island. If we do come to a dead end, the only way we'll be able to get out is by retracing our route, by tacking back and forth against the wind. I'm relieved when our course does, in fact, take another turn, and I proceed deeper into Bair Island.

Another half mile in, it looks like we're approaching what must be another turn, but as we get closer, I realize we may be in trouble.

"Will, is that a turn up ahead?" I ask, despite the fact that I know his guess is as good as mine.

"Uh, I don't think so."

Still slightly optimistic, I sail further on to see if the inlet turns to the right. Then I hear a loud noise.

I know this feeling all too well; we're stuck. The boat's rudder and centerboard are caught in a wet quagmire of mud.

"Thump." Betty suddenly stops, causing both Will and me to fall over into the boat. I know this feeling all too well; we're stuck. The boat's rudder and centerboard are caught in a wet quagmire of mud.

"Oh, damn, we're stuck," I yell.

"Oh, damn, damn," Will repeats.

The little wind blowing is working against us, pushing us deeper and deeper into the undredged marsh. The tan grass now rubs against the boat, entangling Betty. Within minutes, we are completely stuck, miles away from the nearest human beings.

Will says, "Blake, look over there." He points to another, wider inlet, almost parallel to ours, across a narrow strip of bog. I then realize our inlet is not the Corkscrew. We're looking across at the real Corkscrew and at the marshy ground separating us. We can't sail to the Corkscrew, and if we were to try walking across this quagmire, we would sink

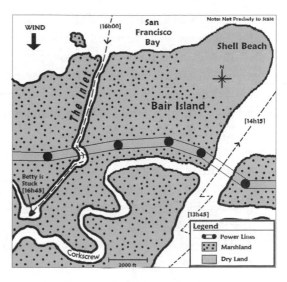

up to our waists. There is also a ten-foot vertical drop on the other side.

"Blake, what are we gonna do?" Will asks. He's clearly worried. His eyes are wide open and his brow is furrowed. His confidence in me has been shaken.

"Umm, let me think..." I've gotten stuck in mud before at the summer camp, and I remember that I used the tiller extension, a two-foot piece of wood, as a lever to force my way out of it. I decide to try it.

We pull up the centerboard and the rudder. By now it's getting close to five o'clock, and I know that by six the sun will be setting, making things worse. What if we're forced to stay in the boat overnight?

I know that I can't simply stick the tiller extension into the mud and then push, for the ground is too soft. I have another idea: I push the tiller extension under the back of the boat at an angle, and then I pull it toward me until it is perpendicular to the boat. Little by little, I inch the boat out of the bamboolike grass, using the tiller extension as a lever.

"Come on, Betty! That's a good girl, keep moving!" I say, as I push the boat along.

The boat plows through about twenty feet of thick grass until we reenter the inlet from which we've come.

"Ugh, we're finally out of that disaster," I say to Will.

"But now we have to sail all the way back up the inlet," he points out.

I'm facing a problem. I'm going to have to tack up two miles of an extremely narrow inlet in almost still-wind conditions. And even when we reach the bay, it's going to be another three miles into port. I glance back at the tiller. That's when I see them, swarming onto the boat.

"Will, look!" I yell. Spiders!"

It's like a nightmare. Four hand-sized spiders, followed by hundreds of small tan-colored spiders, have invaded the boat from the stern. The larger spiders, in the space of a few minutes, have already begun to weave their webs on the sails and on the back corner of the boat.

"Splash them!" Will yells, as he frantically begins scooping up water.

We hang over the sides, splashing water into the boat as fast as we can. We do this for ten minutes until the spiders are floating all around our feet. I wonder if things can get any worse.

If I hadn't happened to look back at the boat's tiller right then, we would have been overrun by spiders, maybe even poisonous ones. Shaken, I return to sailing up the inlet, looking back every minute or so to make sure no more spiders have crawled onto the boat. Since the inlet is so narrow, I have to make hundreds of mini tacks. By now, it's about five thirty, an hour and a half after we were due back into port.

"Blake, those spiders freaked me out," Will says.

Although we are both strong guys who lift weights, we admit to each other that we were both scared of the spiders. As we mini-tack up the inlet, I regret not following the rules of the sailing school, for I am rapidly losing Will's trust.

We don't reach the mouth of the inlet until a quarter of six. Dusk is approaching, and to make matters worse, I know that the water in the bay is about fifty degrees; if we were to capsize, we would have about fifty minutes before hypothermia set in.

"Knowing my mother, she'll probably have every motorboat within the vicinity searching for us," I say. "And, by nightfall, she'll probably send police helicopters and the Coast Guard, too." I am beginning to think that this might not be such a bad idea.

Suddenly, a white motorboat appears around the corner of Shell Beach. Will jumps up and waves. The motorboat I earlier tried so hard to avoid is now coming to our rescue. There is still enough light to see that the man driving the boat is Jay, the sailing director. He is steering the motorboat with a steely arm; his face is red with anger. I know I am in for big trouble and am struggling with what to say when he reaches us.

"Good evening," I say in a friendly tone, trying my best to smile. "Do you have any goddamn sense of what time it is?" he yells. "Do you know what could have happened to both of you out here in the bay at night?"

Will and I are both silent. Jay is right.

"I know, Blake, that you are well aware of the fact that you are not allowed to go past the power lines," he says. "You have a history of trying to go out in the bay. You flagrantly disobeyed the rules."

He pulls up alongside our boat and throws us a yellow rope, which we attach to Betty's mast. Then he begins to haul us in. During the forty-minute ride back, I think about what I've done: how I have disobeyed the rules and what could have happened as a result.

By the time we reach the boathouse, the sun has already set. My mother is waiting on the dock, looking exhausted. She stands like a statue with her arms clutched. She has been too worried and upset to begin scolding me now. Jay sternly lectures Will and me, and even my mother, about the dangers of sailing in the bay: how a small boat could be sucked out by the afternoon tide and through the Golden Gate; how you never sail alone without anyone knowing where you are going; how recently two other boys had been stranded on Bair Island and almost died from hypothermia.

Jay lowers the boom: "Blake, you are banned from sailing here any longer."

As Jay glares, Will and I remove the rigging from Betty, scrub off the marsh mud and hundreds of spiders from inside and outside the boat with brushes, and then put her back inside the boathouse.

When I arrive home, Mimi calls me into her room.

"Blake, I was frantic. No one knew what had happened to both of you. All they told me was that there was a boat missing. Do you know what that feels like? When you are told your son's boat is missing?" she asks.

"No, I don't," I answer.

"Blake, you've been told twenty times not to go into the bay. There is a reason for the rules," she says. She repeats all the reasons.

I hear her, and I know she is right, and I'm sorry I've made her worry. But I am even more upset that I have lost the trust of the entire Stanford sailing school. The school has special memories for me, and now I've been banned from sailing there because I brashly disobeyed the rules. This is a fact that really hurts. When will I learn?

cause & effect

Many people with ADHD have a tendency to be somewhat difficult and tend not to listen to or follow directions. You think the rules are for someone else. You think you can just do what you want to do, and the rules are just annoyances that are in your way and should be ignored. This is what has happened to me on many occasions. I continue to struggle with this problem, as you can see from my recent misadventure on the bay. In situations like this, I always feel that my way of doing things is justified. I guess you can say that I have enough faith in my own judgment and believe that I am right. This attitude has cost me.

I tried to figure out what was going on in my mind during the adventure with Will. First, I believed that the instructors at the sailing school had decided that boats shouldn't be taken into the bay because many of the sailors did not know how to sail well. I felt irritated that they applied the rule to me even though I am a good sailor and should have been allowed the extra privilege. Second, by sailing past the boundary and showing them I could do it successfully, I wanted to prove the instructors wrong. Third, I believed that if I didn't get to sail in the bay, I would have no fun. Last, I wanted to

> I always feel that my way of doing things is justified. This attitude has cost me.

impress my friend by showing him how I could sail in the big bay.

It is the fear of the unknown that motivates me to take charge.

Breaking rules ties in with another tendency of mine, which you may share. I have discovered that I like to control situations. I don't think I'm a control freak, but I always prefer it if I can do something my own way. I fear that if a task or assignment is not done my way, it will turn out badly. In the sailing incident, I thought I knew better than everyone else, the rule makers (the Stanford sailing school), the rule enforcers (Jay, the sailing instructor), and even Will (my friend, who questioned if we should be breaking the rule). I had made up my mind to sail into the bay.

Needing to do things my way also applies to school. In my chemistry and biology labs, I work with two or three lab partners. Almost instinctively, I figure that everyone in the group will follow my procedure for mixing chemicals or dissecting a rat so that the task is completed successfully. I fear that if I follow the suggestions of my lab partners, the lab experiment will fail and consequently we will all receive a bad grade for the lab.

I'm not suggesting that I don't have faith in others' abilities—I just don't know their abilities. It is the fear of the unknown that motivates me to take charge.

But the truth is that although I am right many times, I don't always know best. I've discovered that when I listen to my classmates in chemistry and biology labs, they have many good ideas to improve our experiments and our lab reports. For example, one of my classmates suggested clipping a thermometer to a stand instead of holding it, to make our results more accurate, and our grades ended up being even better.

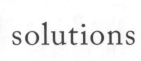

solutions

If you are a rule breaker and tend to think you always know better than everyone else, think again. I've found that it's important to get information and listen to others. Doing so can keep you out of trouble.

① **Get information.** In many cases, you may feel that a rule is pointless. Instead of making assumptions, consider that you may be unaware of certain things. You may be missing some information, as I was when I sailed into the bay. For instance, I didn't know we could get stuck. I didn't know that the current, caused by late afternoon tide, was capable of dragging my boat from the bay through the treacherous Golden Gate. I failed to consider that if you go off without anyone knowing where you are, people will have no way of knowing where to look for you if something bad happens. Rules are usually there for a good reason: to keep order, to prevent harm. Rules are not there to annoy you or restrict you. Rules are there to allow you the freedom to do things safely while taking other people into consideration. If you think about this when confronted by rules, you probably won't be as reluctant to follow them. If you have a question about a rule, ask for the reason behind it.

② **Listen to others.** You may doubt another person's abilities just because you are unaware of their knowledge and talents. There are many intelligent people among your parents, teachers, friends, classmates, and lab partners. Be open to advice, ideas, and discussion. A team is valuable because each person can contribute information, intelligence, wisdom, or a new perspective. When I sailed into the bay against the rules, I wasn't listening to anyone but myself. I was convinced Will and I should sail in the bay. I didn't ask Will's opinion or stop to listen to him when he questioned whether we should be doing it. I had already made up my mind as to what we would do. You should at least hear what other people have to say.

I'm not saying you shouldn't defend your ideas. It's not a black-or-white situation: my way or your way. It can be a combination of the two ways, taking the best of both. As my mother has always said, a truly intelligent person will always ask the questions, get the information, and may even change his or her ideas based on that new information. She also said that wisdom comes in all forms—young, middle-aged, and old, from people of all races and religions. No one has the corner on this market.

③ **Just follow (most of) the rules.** This may seem like the typical, annoying advice you get from your parents or teachers, but you will be better off if you simply follow the rules. I'm not suggesting that you do everything that someone tells you to do, but keep in mind that the rules are there for a reason. Some rules may seem silly, but at least find out why the rule is a rule. Don't just ignore it. If you believe a rule is not justified, get information and ask for an explanation.

So, to return to the moral of my story, follow the rules and hopefully the spiders won't get you!

— 13 —

being discriminated against

the private school interview 8th grade

I open the door of our car and step into the school parking lot. My mother exits from the driver's seat, takes a breath of fresh December air, and sighs. Just then, I feel a tic coming. I have a very strong, semiconscious urge to shake my head. I figure that I should just complete the tic and get it over with. I look around to make sure no one is watching, and I shake my head abruptly. Done, I think, at least for the next ten minutes or so.

I am at a private high school for an interview. Now that I'm in eighth grade, I'm leaving middle school and am applying to different high schools. This interview is the last step in the application process. I have a lot going for me—good grades, a classical instrument, sports—but I also have ADHD.

I walk across the parking lot, followed by my mother. Her heels click on the stone pavement. About a minute later, we step into the neoclassical-style school building. A man in a suit greets us near a portable table covered with neatly stacked papers.

"Hello, how are you today?" he says with what seems like a false smile.

"Very good," I reply for both my mother and me.

"Hi, I'm Nadine," my mother says, shaking his hand. "And this is my son, Blake."

I shake the man's hand.

"Allow me to give you a name tag," he says, reaching over the table to pick up two stickers and a black pen.

We write our names on the blue-and-white stickers and then continue down the hallway. I hear my mother's high heels clicking on the wooden floor. We turn at a sign labeled "Admissions."

"Okay," I think, "if a tic is coming, I had better finish it now." I shake my head to try to preempt the tic. The admissions assistant, who's sitting behind her desk in a white linen suit, looks over at me, a little surprised, as if I need help. Then she motions us to enter the director's office. Since the door is only partially ajar, I push it open further. The director, a matronly women sitting at her desk, swivels away from her computer to greet us.

"Hi," she says, without the courtesy of getting up.

"Hello, I'm Nadine, and this is my son, Blake." The director extends a hand to each of us. Her hand feels cold.

"Okay," she says to my mother, "if you wouldn't mind leaving the room, I'll talk with your son for about thirty minutes."

My mother smiles, clips her sunglasses to her blouse, and leaves the room. So far, so good: no tics. I sit down in the French chair facing the director's desk.

"So, Blake, I'm going to ask you a couple questions. It shouldn't take that long." She swivels her chair around in search of something but seems to have trouble finding it. She finally locates it, but the object is too high for her to reach while seated. Reluctantly, she stands up halfway, removes a clipboard from a shelf, and sits back down. She adjusts her floral skirt while letting out a sigh.

"Okay, so…" She searches on the clipboard and flips the page.

"So, where do you go to school?" She fixes her short dyed-blonde hair behind her ears as she looks over at me.

"I go to Crocker Middle School."

"Oh, Crocker. I friend of mine's daughter goes there, but I think she's in sixth grade."

"Oh," I reply.

"So, do you play an instrument?"

"Yes, classical piano." She tries to write on her clipboard, but her pen runs out of ink. She tosses it down, then sticks her hand into a messy pile of papers on her desk, and, to my surprise, manages to retrieve another pen.

"Tell me more about your playing. Which composers do you play? Have you given recitals?"

I tell her about my love for Mozart, Beethoven, and Chopin and say that I've played in a number of recitals.

"Do you play sports?"

"Yes, I do. Swimming, skiing, sailing, and tennis."

We talk more about my experience on the ski team and my summer camp in sailing.

She looks impressed. As she makes a note of this, I feel the tic coming. Not here, I say to my subconscious. But my subconscious won't obey. The tic is on its way.

"So, what do you do in your free time?" She looks at me and then at the clock to her right.

"Well, a wide variety of things. I do a lot of greyhound rescue work. Sometimes I bike, sometimes I design and launch model rockets, umm…" I keep going. "I walk, construct towers and transportation systems, I go to the gym, uh…"

While I am thinking of other accomplishments to tell her about, she says, "I think I have plenty of information." She crosses her legs and makes another note to herself.

I feel the tic again. I have to do it now. Yes, it is coming, and there is nothing I can do to stop it. I want to stop it, but I can't. I feel like I am waging a war with myself.

While she is looking down, I try to quickly shake my head, but as I am doing this, she finishes writing and looks up at me, staring. There is an awkward silence. She saw the tic, I saw her see the tic, and, unlike a cough or a sneeze, there is no explanation for why I've abruptly shaken my head.

"Excuse me, but is everything all right?" she is bold enough to ask.

"Yes, just my neck hurts from yesterday," I say, realizing it's a lame excuse.

She looks at her clipboard in disbelief. I know she doesn't buy my excuse. Now she probably thinks I'm strange. And why should someone who is strange be admitted into this prestigious school?

She seems anxious to finish the interview, and after some pleasantries, I stand up and I shake her hand while she remains seated. We say our good-byes, and I leave the room. My mother is on the other side of the hallway, reading a magazine. She looks up at me.

"So, how did it go, honey?" she asks as she attempts to give me a hug. I pull away.

"Good, good," I say. There will be twenty-five minutes in the car to explain what happened in the director's office.

Suddenly, a short, black-haired woman appears with a tray of cookies and offers us one. I take one and my mother politely declines. It's a brittle cookie, not the soft kind that I like, and after taking a small bite, I throw it into the trash. As my mother and I leave the building, we pass the man in the suit.

"See you later," he says, smiling at us again with that insincere smile. But considering the tic that I had during my interview, I figure he won't be seeing us. There will be no "later" at this school.

"Okay, bye now," my mother replies for both of us.

We exit the building. This time, my mother's white heels are clicking in front of me.

cause  effect

I found out later that the director of admissions called my mother after the interview and abruptly asked if I had Tourette's syndrome, a chronic tic disorder in which a person has physical and verbal tics. My mother explained that I have ADHD, which I talked about in my application, but not Tourette's. She explained that my doctor had specifically examined me for Tourette's and found that I had a simple tic disorder, which comes out especially when I am nervous.

My mother went on to explain that my doctor was in the process of changing my medication. The director evidently did not believe my mother, for she then requested that my doctor send a letter directly to her with the diagnosis. My doctor confirmed all of this in her letter.

One month later, I received a rejection letter from the school.

I believe I was rejected from this school because of the tics associated with my ADHD. I had been honest about the fact that I had ADHD and the steps I have taken to manage it, but it obviously wasn't enough. I thought to myself, "This is the kind of thing we read about in our schoolbooks." All the different kinds of discrimination: against the Irish and Italians during the years between the wars or toward women and black Americans fighting for equal rights in the 1960s. Those prejudices seemed remote and almost old-fashioned when I read about them, but this happened to me in 2003! This happened in the liberal, forward-thinking, socially conscious San Francisco Bay Area. I was stunned. Despite my good grades, sports, and other activities, I believe I was rejected because I shook my head at the wrong time.

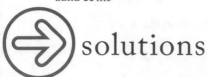 solutions

You may find that you are discriminated against because you have ADHD. Here is my best advice for how to handle discrimination.

(1) **Understand that bias exists.** Realize that you will come up against bias. It is a fact of life for many people and for people with ADHD. You may not be able to change the way certain institutions or people think, but you can change how you react to it. Have confidence in yourself and your abilities.

(2) **Go to a school where differences are respected and accepted.** Some schools are not tolerant of differences, and others are. You want to be in a place where you are respected for your abilities, not looked down upon because of your condition. This will make all the difference in how you feel about yourself and in how your classmates react to you. You want to be in a school that will bring out the best in you, where you will be engaged and nurtured.

I found supportive people in both public and private schools. These people cared about me. They saw my talents, and they put me in a position to use my talents and to excel at critical times in my life. At Hurlbutt Elementary School, in Weston, Connecticut, my principal, the much-admired Dr. Tomasello (or Dr. T) noticed that I was hyperactive, but he also noticed that I had a passion for geography, and he invited me to do an independent study project on Europe with him in second grade. When I was in fifth grade at the Weston Middle School, Mrs. Motroni gave us many reports and history presentations to do. She was a tough teacher,

> You may not be able to change the way certain institutions or people think, but you can change how you react to it.

but I respected her and wanted to do good work for her. I excelled in her class. Mark Tangerone and Elaine Pawlowski, two teachers who ran a special class for gifted students at this school, channeled my curiosity into special projects on the planets, space probes, and high-speed trains.

At Crocker Middle School, in Hillsborough, California, Janet Chun, principal, and Susan Camarillo, school counselor, encouraged my work as the Crocker TV weatherman on the school's daily news program for students. They allowed me to be creative, to do weather trivia for the entire school, and Troy Hager taught me how to produce weather features for the news program. As a result, my classmates saw what I was capable of doing and suddenly thought differently of me, and I found my place among them.

Finally, at the French-American International School's high school in San Francisco, a terrific teacher of English and theory of knowledge, Dan Harder, read the first chapters for this book and encouraged me to continue: "You have something very important to say, and you have a unique voice. A book like this will help other young people. Keep writing!" I appreciated his constant encouragement, along with his humor and sharp wit. I even learned how to read his illegible handwriting. He edited my writing, we argued about using "SAT" words, and he motivated me to do what I thought was impossible—writing a book.

You need to find the right place for you and the right people, who will have faith in you, to help bring out your hidden talents. Thank goodness I was declined by the high school in this story. If I'd gone to that school, I would never have accomplished so much.

taking control

the revolution 10th grade

"No! I don't want it cut short," I yell at my mother in a hair salon on Martha's Vineyard. We are on vacation, and my mother, grandmother, and sister Madison have decided that it's time to make me change my hairstyle.

"You're cutting it shorter, and that's it," my mother replies firmly.

The young hair stylist with purple hair holds the scissors above my head, hesitating to begin cutting because of the argument.

"Look, you should just get it cut shorter. It'll look better," Madison says with her arms crossed.

I am terrified—I have had the same haircut since I was two years of age, and am not, for anything, willing to try a new style thirteen years later, now that I'm fifteen. I look at the scissors apprehensively.

My grandmother, who is wearing a denim blazer, chimes in, "Blakey, I think you should try a more adult style. Why don't you listen to your mother?"

"I don't want it cut that way! What if it looks worse?"

The hairdresser, who has other customers waiting in line, intervenes.

"Honey, it won't look worse," she reassures me. "I've been cutting hair for ten years, and everyone likes my haircuts."

She fingers the wet locks of my hair in preparation.

"Look, all the good-looking guys in my school have short hair, and they gel it up in the front. You should get it cut short too," my sister says.

There is a long, awkward silence during which I think about my bowl haircut and how I have not received any compliments about it for a long time. I then think of guys in my school with their hair gelled and how they have no trouble in finding girls to dance with at the school parties. With this in mind, I decide that perhaps I should finally change my haircut.

Somewhat reluctantly, I say, "Okay, fine. Cut my hair short."

I then inhale a breath of summer beach air.

After forty minutes of intense combing and cutting, the hairdresser has completed her task. She puts some gel in my hair, making it stand up in front. I reach for my glasses and put them on. I look in the mirror.

"Not too bad…," I think to myself as I touch my hair.

It's at that very moment that I begin the journey to change myself. It is time for a revolution.

cause & effect

I began to change when I realized it was up to me. I had to make the conscious decision to change myself; it was not going to happen by itself.

It was all in my hands, as it is in yours. So, I began what I like to call "the revolution," in which slowly but surely I began to change many aspects about myself. Gradually, over two years, I changed my appearance and became more fit, I became more organized in my schoolwork and at home, I became part of the social scene at school, I involved myself more in community service work, I pursued my classical piano playing with a passion, and I started a part-time job on Saturdays. The more I did, the more positive the response. The more positive the response, the more confident I became. I became very happy within myself. It may seem obvious that you have a lot of control over your life, but often people miss the obvious.

solutions

I once got a fortune cookie that read, "You constantly struggle for self-improvement." It stated my goals so well, I've kept it in a prominent place on a bulletin board over my desk. Though everyone with ADHD is different, we all can gain from taking charge of our individual situations. And even if your situation and issues are different from mine, I'm sure we have things in common. Here are some of my solutions.

(1) **If something's not working, change it.** At the end of ninth grade, I had glasses and a blond bowl-style haircut and no sense of style whatsoever. Initially, I did not think much of looks and style, considering them to be superficial and unnecessary. I wanted to be good-looking (after all who doesn't?) but was uncertain if it were even a possibility. Even if it were a possibility, I was uncertain of how to go about becoming good-looking. My mother had told me that I was good-looking, but I was convinced that she just said that because she was my

I once got a fortune cookie that read, "You constantly struggle for self-improvement."

mother. On vacation in Martha's Vineyard, my mother, grandmother, and sister, all together, finally convinced me to cut my hair short. Once we took away the bowl, some interesting things began to happen; my perspective changed, and so did I.

During another summer, my luggage was lost and so were all of my boring T-shirts and cargo pants. When we went shopping at the Gap for clothes to replace the ones that were lost, we bought new khaki slacks, jeans, collared shirts, and jackets. I was instantly in style, and, again, I got a positive response to the change. Then it dawned on me: if I could improve my looks, people would like me more.

The revolution continued. For my sixteenth birthday, I asked for contact lenses so that I would no longer have to wear glasses and look nerdy. I got the contacts and things got increasingly better. As I mentioned before, I had started going to the gym to exercise after my mother forced me to go. It soon became part of my regimen and part of the revolution.

My first steps in the revolution were met with success. As I became better looking, I started becoming more popular. As I became more popular, I was more relaxed about myself and about being around other people. I could be happy within myself, and the teasing from classmates ended. As the teasing ended, my self-esteem grew by leaps and bounds. So, this is not to say that I no longer have any ADHD behaviors, but now my classmates generally overlook them. My classmates are interested in me as an individual.

② **Join the social scene.** Changing my looks was only one part of the revolution. In tenth grade, I also made a conscious decision to join the social scene at school. As I mentioned earlier, I figured that if I could show that I was friendly, my classmates would become my friends. I began by joining others at lunchtime; later, we began going shopping after school. During our time together, we had great teenage discussions, about our teachers, and about how to become increasingly independent from our parents. I learned more about them and their personal lives, which made us all closer as friends. We began to hang out together on Fridays after school in downtown San Francisco, taking in movies.

I started going to dances, parties, and gatherings in the city. While doing so, I met friends of friends. We shared experiences that we would discuss at the lunch table days later. Basically, I got into the mainstream of things at school.

I joined the swim team in the spring of tenth grade. Joining a sports team was important. Not only was it healthy, but it also put me into the middle of school life. Suddenly, other classmates were interested in how fast my freestyle and breaststroke times were, and I found a whole new group of friends.

③ **Become active in your community.** Even before my revolution began, during seventh grade I had already become involved in greyhound rescue work. I decided to do my part in the community after our family adopted a former racing greyhound we named Odette, soon followed by two other greyhounds, Persephone and Athena. We learned from the Greyhound Protection League about how twenty thousand greyhounds need to be adopted each year, and we began to do a lot of work on weekends for the greyhound rescue organization Greyhound Friends for Life. We went with other greyhound families and our dogs to fairs and big events, such as the Palo Alto Concours d' Élegance and the Half Moon Bay Pumpkin Festival, set up information booths, and talked to hundreds of people about greyhound adoption. I worked with Petco on greyhound adoption days and their annual Greyhound Planet Week fund-raiser at the San Mateo, California, store. I created a PowerPoint presentation describing the greyhounds' ancient history, their life in racing, the aftermath, and the wonderful work of the rescue groups. This presentation is used by our rescue group for many speaking engagements. In this way, I began to think beyond my immediate self and helped save one life at a time.

④ **Find an outlet for your creativity.** Classical piano has been important to me for six years. It is soothing and helps calm me when I am feeling hyperactive. The music also helps organize my mind when I need to study. Pursuing an instrument or another art is a wonderful outlet for your creativity.

⑤ **Work in the real world.** Getting my first job—a part-time job at Banana Republic—as a sales associate taught me about business and how to deal with the general public. It helped me grow up a lot. Suddenly, I came to understand the value of money; if something cost $30.00, it would mean that I would have to work hours to earn the money to buy it. I've learned how stores market to their customers and how to help customers select clothing. I've learned how small details can have an impact on sales. Sweaters need to be neatly stacked, music played, and cologne sprayed in the store. (And how you never tell a woman she needs a larger size!) Accessories need to be displayed next to basic skirts, jackets, and shirts, to encourage customers to buy entire outfits. I feel good when customers take my advice. For instance, one woman came in looking for a summer blouse, and I was able to help her buy a complete weekend outfit. The customer later told my manager that I was an enthusiastic sales associate.

As my fortune cookie says, I'm in for a lifetime of self-improvement, and that is all right because I like the results so far. You need to decide which steps you want to take for your own personal "revolution."

— 15 —

being gifted
the Ferrari 3rd grade

My mother and I pretend that each person in our family is a car.

"What are you?" I ask my mother. I am nine years old at the time.

"I have a lot of energy. I think I'm a BMW," my mother says. "Madison, too."

"What about Daddy?"

"Your father isn't as fast; we'll make him an Audi."

"What about me?"

"Oh, you," she says. "You are different but really special. You are a bright red Ferrari!"

I love Ferraris. I smile. "What makes me a Ferrari?"

"Your inexhaustible energy and speed," she says. "You, Blake, are the only person in the whole world who can exhaust me."

I think this is pretty good. I can exhaust my mother. She goes on to say that Ferraris are highly tuned for speed and, because of that fact, are more sensitive machines.

"They are extraordinary machines. They are very handsome. They have very powerful engines. But there is a downside," she warns.

I am thinking, how can there be any downside to being a Ferrari?

"You have to know how to control the horsepower in the engine," my mother says. "Sometimes, you speed straight down roads, faster than all the other cars. But other times, you are not watching where you're going, and you zigzag totally out of control. You have to get control of your engine."

"Just think," my mother says, "when you are able to control your Ferrari engine. Imagine the possibilities. Imagine what you will be able to accomplish with this gift."

I thought about it then, and I think about it now. My mother was right, and she always made me feel wonderful.

cause & effect

When I was first diagnosed with ADHD at five years old, I was surprised and scared. My parents did not want to tell me that I had to take medicine for the condition, so they told me instead that my daily medicine was a vitamin. They did not want me to feel as if something were wrong. Also, ADHD was not well-known at the time, twelve years ago.

When I was very young, many people did not believe that such a condition existed. They blamed my mother for my behaviors. They said that she worked too long at her IBM office in New York and traveled on business too much in the United States and in Europe and didn't spend enough time with me. They said that, as a result, my childhood lacked both discipline and attention. Other people said that I behaved the way I did because she was too lenient with me, letting me get away with leaving Legos all over the family room floor or stringing cable cars down the entire hallway from the kitchen to the bedrooms. Conversely, others said that she was too hard on me when she gave me time-outs and that my hyperactive behavior was my way of retaliating. Some said she was too easy on me and complimented me too much, making too big a fuss when I made my bed or got a good grade on a test. Still others believed that I was spoiled and that ADHD was just an excuse that was allowing me to get away with bad behavior. As a result, there wasn't a lot of sympathy.

Even today, I am often flabbergasted by the fact that there are still many people who don't believe ADHD is real. They believe it is a made-up condition and figure it is a way for parents to excuse an unruly child. Often, when I tell people that I have ADHD, they look at me skeptically, as if thinking, "Yeah, sure." Some believe that it is just boys being boys, or boys being difficult. There are other people who will argue that the drug companies created ADHD so that they can sell their medicines. But ADHD is a fact, and it is very real.

Once you accept the fact that ADHD is a real thing, there is the issue of what to call it. Many people call ADHD a "disability," a "disease," or a "disorder." Years ago, doctors referred to it as a "hyperkinetic impulsive disorder," later as a "minimal brain dysfunction." Now, the proper name is attention-deficit/hyperactivity disorder.

No wonder we feel the way we do! Look at what they call our condition. The word "deficit" alone makes us feel as if we are missing something or that something is not working correctly. The word "disorder" makes us feel as if we are flawed, and we think that because we are flawed, we are destined to fail. We believe we are less than other kids, that we are not good enough. When you feel this way, your self-esteem plummets, and you feel less worthy as a person (Honos-Webb 2005).

There are still many people who don't believe ADHD is real. They believe it is a made-up condition and figure it is a way for parents to excuse an unruly child.

Well, we need to change this right here and now. ADHD means we are different. Our brains work differently. It is like being blue-eyed or left-handed. It is just a normal part of the human spectrum. The condition describes the unique way our brains are wired; it does *not* mean that our brains function incorrectly. Doctors Edward Hallowell, a former Harvard Medical School instructor, and John Ratey, an associate professor of psychiatry at Harvard Medical School, both renowned experts on ADHD, said the "best way to think of ADHD is not as a mental disorder but as a collection of traits and tendencies that define a way of being in the world" (2005).

ADHD has many great qualities! Sometimes kids don't realize this fact, but the very traits that make ADHD difficult to live with when you are very young also make it a gift as you get older. As Lara Honos-Webb said in her book, ADHD kids are "different and in a way that our culture has not learned to fully appreciate" (Honos-Webb 2005, 5). If you are hyperactive, as many ADHD individuals are, you have boundless energy to pursue many things. For instance, you can channel that energy into taking more classes than the average student, performing well on sports teams, playing an instrument, or finding the hours to actively participate in community service or in the arts and still have time for your friends. You have more energy than most people. You can accomplish more in a day.

If you are easily distracted, you have a harder time concentrating. But, unlike those who are not easily distracted, you automatically think outside of the box.

If you are impulsive, you often make decisions without thoroughly thinking of the consequences. Don't let the negative side fool you, however; if you are impulsive, you also have an ability to be innovative, to take risks, and to try new approaches when everyone else is doing the same old things. If you are passionate about a subject or an activity, you will be able to pursue it tenaciously.

If you are easily distracted, you have a harder time concentrating. But, unlike those who are not easily distracted, you automatically think outside of the box. You notice everything and are more innovative because your mind is more expansive, and you can find creative and often unorthodox methods to solve a problem. You are also extremely perceptive and can pick up details that others don't see.

If you are overly sensitive, this characteristic makes you more in tune with those around you, more caring, and more understanding. You have an intuition about people, a keen perception. You are more aware of what they are feeling and have more empathy for them. Your feelings run very deep.

Dr. Hallowell said, "ADHD is common among creative and intuitive people in all fields and among highly energetic, interesting, productive people. You can find high stimulation in being a surgeon, or a trial attorney, or an actor, or a pilot, or a trader on the commodities exchange, or working in a newsroom, or in sales, or in being a race car driver!" (2005, 25).

☺ your gifts

Instead of giving you solutions here, as I've done in all the other chapters, I'm going to tell you about all your good qualities. This is not only my opinion. It is also that of doctors and researchers who have found that these qualities are characteristic of people with ADHD (National Resource Center on ADHD 2007; Honos-Webb 2005). So, keep this list on your mirror. Here are some qualities you probably didn't even know you have:

Intelligence. You may learn differently, but you are intelligent. (When I took notes in class, I would color-code them and use figures for key facts which allowed me to learn the material in a different but much better way.)

Charm. You have interpersonal charm, an enthusiasm that people love. (I love having friends over for long dinners and entertaining them with stories and movies.)

A sense of humor. You see the humor and irony in daily life, and you love to point it out to people. (I like to tease my mother about her hundreds of family photos of me and my sister.)

Great energy. You have an abundance of energy, and the secret is to channel it into many, many pursuits: academics, community service, sports, social activities, and other interests. (I got a sense of satisfaction being able to handle seven academic courses, classical piano, part-time work, and swim team. It was a test to see if I could do it.)

An ability to focus intensely on your interests. You have a unique ability to hyperfocus, to work for hours on end on a project or to diligently study something you love. (I spent twenty-five hours once on a paper-mâché sculpture and one hundred hours on an IB extended essay. When I find a subject I like, I can pour an immense amount of time and energy into it, almost effortlessly.)

An ability to do a lot of things at once. You can study history, do IM, talk to your sibling, watch a program on bridge construction, or do any number of other things, all at the same time.

Creativity. You are full of new ideas and have the ability to connect facts and observations in original ways. You have the ability to see things that others don't see, and you ask questions that others haven't thought about. You can be very artistic. (I devised a new breathing apparatus for a biology lab, and I used a lot of graphic design for my math assessment presentation on matrices.)

Compassion and empathy. You have the ability to put yourself in another person's shoes and understand what he or she is feeling. Events make an impact on you. You genuinely feel for people. For example, I've often thought about my great-grandmother Zaira, alone on a ship with a newborn baby and hundreds of other immigrants, sailing from Trieste, to join my great-grandfather Anthony here. Only to face the Depression once here. I think about the sacrifices they made.

Passion. You know what you love in life—a subject, a cause, an occupation, an activity—and you pursue it wholeheartedly. (Biology and chemistry are my passions.)

Trustworthiness and sincerity. You make a very good friend. You are loyal and aren't swayed by what others say. You know the true value in people.

Honesty. You speak truthfully, and people can always depend on this.

An adventurous spirit. You have a spirit for adventure, but you must watch this trait so that you don't get into trouble (as I did during the sailing trip with Will) or get hurt.

Determination. You know what is right. You know what you want. Sometimes you need to temper this with good and important information coming from others. You have to realize that you don't know it all.

A love for animals and nature. You respect and honor the natural world and all its creatures. (Walker 2005). (I work hard for greyhound rescue, endlessly telling people about the need to adopt these gentle, loving animals.)

Remember, ADHD is a gift that makes you different, and like the Ferrari, it makes you one in a million!

references

Adesman, A. 2003. A diagnosis of ADHD? Don't overlook the probability of comorbidity! *Contemporary Pediatrics* 20 (12): 91–106.

American Academy of Family Physicians. 2007. Autism and your child. www.familydoctor.org

American Psychiatric Association. 2000. *Diagnostic and Statistical Manual of Mental Disorders*, 4th edition, text revision. Washington, DC: APA.

Alexander-Roberts, C. 1995. *ADHD and Teens*. Lanham, MD: Taylor Trade Publishing.

Barkley, R. 1998. *Attention-Deficit Hyperactivity Disorder: A Handbook for Diagnosis and Treatment*, 2nd edition. New York: Guilford Press.

Biederman, J., S.V. Faraone, and K. Lapey. 1992. Comorbidity of diagnosis in attention deficit disorders. In *Child and Adolescent Psychiatric Clinics of North America: Attention Deficit Hyperactivity Disorder*, edited by G. Weiss. Philadelphia: Saunders.

Borba, M. 2006. Bullying. Lecture delivered at Hillsborough School District Headquarters, Hillsborough, California, May 3.

Carey, B. 2006. What's wrong with a child? Psychiatrists often disagree. *New York Times*, November 11, 1.

CDC. September 2, 2005. *Morbidity and Mortality Weekly Report*. 54: 842-847. News release, CDC.

Gaab, N. 2006. Exploring the musical brain. Lecture delivered at Cupertino, California, October 14.

Graham, J. 2006. Can't focus? Why your thoughts wander. *Good Housekeeping Magazine*, January, 54.

Greyhound Protection League. 2007. http://greyhounds.org.

Hallowell, E., and J. Ratey. 2005. *Delivered from Distraction*. New York: Ballantine Books.

Honos-Webb, L. 2005. *The Gift of ADHD*. Oakland, CA: New Harbinger Publications.

Kuo, F. E., and A. Faber Taylor. 2004. A potential natural treatment for attention-deficit/hyperactivity disorder: Evidence from a national study. *American Journal of Public Health* 94 (9): 1580-1586.

Lynn, G. 1996. *Survival Strategies For Parenting Your ADD Child*. Grass Valley, CA: Underwood Books, Inc.

National Resource Center on ADHD. 2007. http://www.help4adhd.org/

Pliszka, S. R., C. L. Carlson, and J. M. Swanson. 1999. *ADHD with Comorbid Disorders: Clinical Assessment and Management*. New York: Guilford Press.

PBS *Frontline*. 2007. Medicating Kids: Interview with Russell Barkley. http://www.pbs.org/wgbh/pages/frontline/shows/medicating/interviews/barkley.html.

Walker, B. 2005. *The Girl's Guide to AD/HD*. Bethesda, MD: Woodbine House.

Woods, D. W., R.G. Miltenberger, and V.A. Lumley. 1996. Sequential application of major habit-reversal components to treat motor tics in children. *Journal of Applied Behavior Analysis* 29, 483-493.

Zeigler Dendy, C., and A. Zeigler. 2003. *A Bird's Eye View of Life with ADD and ADHD*. Cedar Bluff, AL: Cherish the Children.

Blake E. S. Taylor is a freshman at the University of California, Berkeley. He wrote *ADHD and Me* during his last two years in high school. Taylor was the recipient of the UC Berkeley California Alumni Association Leadership Award for outstanding student leadership outside the classroom.

Foreword writer **Lara Honos-Webb, Ph.D.,** is California psychologist specializing in ADHD and depression. She is author of *The Gift of ADHD, Listening to Depression, The Gift of ADHD Activity Book,* and the forthcoming *Gift of Adult ADHD.*